미국교과서 리스닝 with DICTATION

Level 3

오석태 지음

길벗스쿨

저자 **오석태**

한국 외국어대학교에서 한국어와 영어를 전공하고, 학생들의 영어 실력 향상을 위해 자신만의
영어 노하우를 개발하며 강의를 했다. 1988년 KBS FM Radio를 통해 방송계에 입문하면서 TV
와 라디오에서 활동하는 방송영어 스타로 자리매김했으며, 2008년부터 영어 콘텐츠 개발 전문
저자로 활동하며 ELC Contents라는 출판사 겸 콘텐츠 개발 전문회사를 설립하였다. 현재 ELC
Contents의 영어교재 출판 상표(imprint)인 OST English를 통해 책을 출간하고 있다.

저서 〈미드가 들리는 리스닝 트레이닝〉, 〈영어는 입으로〉, 〈영어 회화의 결정적 표현들〉,
〈오석태의 영어회화 끝장 레슨〉, 〈악마는 프라다를 입는다 자막없이 보기〉,
〈영어회화 끝장패턴〉, 〈오석태의 말하는 영어〉, 〈영어회화 무작정 따라하기〉,
〈미국교과서 READING〉 등

❙ 일러두기
〈미국교과서 리스닝 with DICTATION〉은 2013년 출간된 〈기적의 미국교과서 받아쓰기〉의 개정판입니다.

미국교과서 리스닝 with DICTATION Level 3
American Textbook Listening with DICTATION Level 3

초판 발행 · 2020년 9월 30일

지은이 · 오석태
발행인 · 이종원
발행처 · 길벗스쿨
출판사 등록일 · 2006년 7월 1일 | **주소** · 서울시 마포구 월드컵로 10길 56 (서교동)
대표 전화 · 02)332-0931 | **팩스** · 02)323-0586
홈페이지 · www.gilbutschool.co.kr | **이메일** · gilbut@gilbut.co.kr

기획 및 책임 편집 · 이경희, 김미경(moon@gilbut.co.kr) | **디자인** · 박찬진, 윤미주 | **제작** · 이진혁
영업마케팅 · 김진성, 박선경 | **웹마케팅** · 박달님, 권은나 | **영업관리** · 정경화 | **독자지원** · 송혜란, 홍혜진

전산편집 · 윤미주 | **본문삽화** · 배성환, 양지원, 김태균, 박기종
인쇄 · 벽호 | **제본** · 벽호 | **녹음** · YR 미디어

ISBN 979-11-6406-263-8 64740 (길벗 도서번호 30491)
　　　979-11-6406-260-7 64740 (세트)
정가 13,000원

독자의 1초를 아껴주는 정성 길벗출판사
길벗 | IT실용서, IT/일반 수험서, IT전문서, 경제실용서, 취미실용서, 건강실용서, 자녀교육서
더퀘스트 | 인문교양서, 비즈니스서
길벗이지톡 | 어학단행본, 어학수험서
길벗스쿨 | 국어학습서, 수학학습서, 유아학습서, 어학학습서, 어린이교양서, 교과서

길벗스쿨 공식 카페 〈기적의 공부방〉 · cafe.naver.com/gilbutschool
인스타그램 / 카카오플러스친구 · @gilbutschool

제 품 명 : 미국교과서 리스닝
　　　　with DICTATION Level 3
제조사명 : 길벗스쿨
제조국명 : 대한민국
전화번호 : 02-332-0931
주　소 : 서울시 마포구 월드컵로
　　　　10길 56 (서교동)
제조년월 : 판권에 별도 표기
사용연령 : **11세 이상**
KC마크는 이 제품이 공통안전기준에
적합하였음을 의미합니다.

미국교과서 듣기 & 받아쓰기를 통한 영어 실력 업그레이드

미국교과서는 영어 보물창고

미국 초등학교 교과서로 영어를 공부하는 학생들이 늘어나면서 이제 미국교과서는 영어 리딩을 위한 필수 과정이 된 것 같습니다. 과학, 사회, 예체능 과목의 지문을 읽으며 교과 지식과 영어를 동시에 공부하는 것은 선생님과 학생들에게 좋은 영어 학습인 것은 분명합니다. 하지만 미국교과서를 리딩으로만 배우기에는 한계가 있습니다.

영어 공부에 왕도는 없지만, 정도는 있습니다. 바르고 좋은 문장을 많이 외우는 것입니다. 문장을 외우는 가장 좋은 방법은 반복적으로 듣고, 따라 말하고, 받아쓰는 것입니다. 미국교과서는 좋은 문장으로 가득 찬 보물창고로, 가장 정확하고 세련된 현대적인 영어 표현을 배울 수 있습니다. 이를 외우고 활용한다면 학생들은 자신만의 영어 보물창고를 갖게 될 것입니다.

단계적으로 접근하는 듣기, 받아쓰기

이 교재의 최종 학습 목표는 과목별로 한 단락에서 두 단락 분량의 교과서 지문을 통으로 외우는 것입니다. 교과서 지문을 외우는 과정이 지겹고 고통스럽지 않도록 여섯 단계로 구성되어 있습니다. 먼저 단어와 문장을 따라 말하는 연습을 합니다. 다음에는 단어와 문장을 듣고 받아쓰는 연습을 합니다. 이 과정을 거치면 기본 단어와 문장을 저절로 암기하게 됩니다. 다음 단계는 앞에서 배운 단어와 문장이 반복적으로 나타나는 짧은 문장과 대화문을 듣고 받아쓰는 훈련을 합니다. 마지막으로 지금까지 배운 모든 표현이 들어가 있는 교과서 지문을 듣고 받아씁니다. 마지막 단계를 마치게 되면 학습자는 교과서 지문을 통으로 외우는 수준이 될 것입니다.

교과서를 듣고, 받아쓰는 과정에서 영어 듣기는 물론 머릿속에 입력된 영어 문장들은 자연스럽게 쓰기와 말하기에도 도움이 될 것입니다.

이 책으로 학생들이 좋은 영어 문장을 맛보고 알아가는 즐거움을 느끼고, 이를 통해 영어 공부에 자신감을 얻을 수 있기를 바랍니다.

오석태

주제 확인

듣고 받아쓸 교과 과목 및 지문의 주제를 확인합니다. 공부하기 전에 주제에 대해서 한 번 생각해 보고 학습에 들어가면 학습 효과도 높고 학습한 내용도 오래 기억할 수 있습니다.

핵심단어 따라 말하기

받아쓸 주제와 관련된 핵심단어 10개를 듣고 따라 말해 봅니다. 각 단어를 3회씩 들려줍니다. 원어민의 음성을 듣고 따라 말하면서 단어의 정확한 발음과 의미를 익혀 보세요.

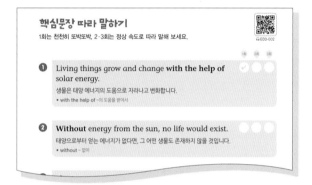

핵심문장 따라 말하기

받아쓸 교과 지문의 주요 내용이 포함된 핵심문장 4개를 듣고 따라 말해 봅니다. 각 문장을 느린 속도와 정상 속도로 3회 들려줍니다. 연음과 억양에 주의하면서 원어민의 음성을 듣고 따라 말해 보세요.

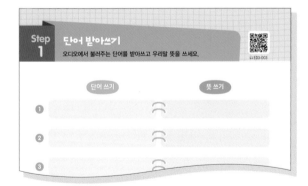

단어 받아쓰기

〈핵심단어 따라 말하기〉에서 연습한 10개 단어를 듣고 받아쓰는 단계입니다. 원어민이 불러주는 영어 단어를 듣고 영어 단어와 그 의미를 써 보세요.

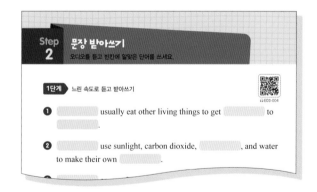

문장 받아쓰기

〈핵심문장 따라 말하기〉에서 연습한 4개의 문장을 듣고 받아쓰는 단계입니다. 1단계에서는 천천히 읽어주는 문장을 듣고 문장 속 단어 1~2개를 받아쓰고, 2단계에서는 정상 속도로 읽어주는 문장을 듣고 문장 속 단어 2~4개를 쓰면 됩니다.

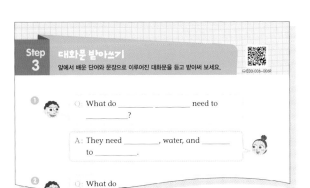

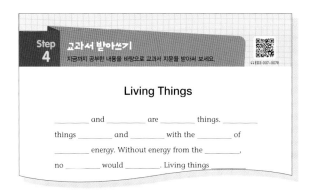

대화문 받아쓰기

배운 단어와 문장을 이용해서 두 사람이 대화를 나눕니다. 받아쓸 때는 받아쓰기용 MP3 파일을 이용하고, 잘 받아 적었는지 확인하거나 다시 듣고 싶을 때는 파일명에 R자가 붙은 복습용 MP3 파일을 이용하면 됩니다.

교과서 받아쓰기

오늘 배운 주제와 관련된 교과서 지문이 제시됩니다. 앞 단계에서 배운 단어, 문장이 빈칸으로 되어 있습니다. 잘 듣고 빈칸을 채우면서 교과서 지문을 완성합니다. 받아쓸 때는 받아쓰기용 MP3 파일을 이용하고, 잘 받아 적었는지 확인하거나 다시 듣고 싶을 때는 파일명에 R자가 붙은 복습용 MP3 파일을 이용하면 됩니다.

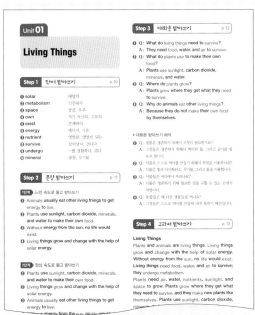

정답 및 해석

본문 문제들의 정답 및 스크립트, 대화문과 지문에 대한 우리말 해석을 수록하였습니다. 정답 및 해석이 되지 않는 문장들의 의미를 확인하면서 다시 한번 생각하고 점검해 볼 수 있습니다.

QR코드

스마트폰의 QR코드 인식기능을 활용하여 해당 음원을 쉽게 들을 수 있습니다. 또한 홈페이지(www.gilbutschool.co.kr)에서도 MP3 파일을 무료로 다운받으실 수 있습니다.

온라인 부가자료

Word List, Word Test, Key Sentence Writing 등 다양한 부가 학습자료를 홈페이지(www.gilbutschool.co.kr)에서 무료로 다운받으실 수 있습니다.

Science

Unit 01 Living Things 8

Unit 02 Leaves, Stems, and Roots ... 14

Unit 03 Flowers, Seeds, and Fruits ... 20

Unit 04 All Kinds of Animals 26

Unit 05 What Animals Need to Live ... 32

Unit 06 What Animals Eat 38

Social Studies

Unit 07 Families and Changes 44

Unit 08 Changing Communities 50

Unit 09 Many Jobs 56

Unit 10 Producers and Consumers ... 62

Unit 11 Egypt 68

Unit 12 The Nile 74

Music

Unit 13 An Orchestra ········· 80

Unit 14 Great Composers and a Symphony ········· 86

Unit 15 Opera ········· 92

Unit 16 Ballet ········· 98

Arts

Unit 17 Shapes ········· 104

Unit 18 Portraits ········· 110

Unit 19 Self-Portraits ········· 116

Unit 20 Still Lifes ········· 122

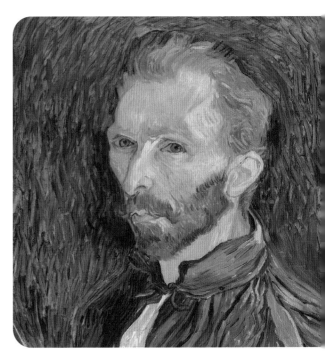

Unit 01 Living Things

* 식물과 동물의 신진대사에 대한 표현을 듣고 받아써 봅니다.

핵심단어 따라 말하기

단어를 3회 들려줍니다. 한 번씩 듣고 따라 말해 보세요.

🎧 ED3-001

		1회	2회	3회
❶ **exist** [igzíst]	통 존재하다	✔		
❷ **solar** [sóulər]	형 태양의			
❸ **metabolism** [mətǽbəlìzəm]	명 신진대사			
❹ **undergo** [ʌndərgóu]	통 ~를 경험하다, 겪다			
❺ **survive** [sərváiv]	통 살아남다, 견디다			
❻ **mineral** [mínərəl]	명 광물, 무기물			
❼ **nutrient** [njú:triənt]	명 영양분 형 영양이 되는			
❽ **space** [speis]	명 공간, 우주			
❾ **own** [oun]	형 자기 자신의, 고유의			
❿ **energy** [énərʒi]	명 에너지, 기운			

핵심문장 따라 말하기

1회는 천천히 또박또박, 2·3회는 정상 속도로 따라 말해 보세요.

🎧 ED3-002

1회   2회   3회

1 Living things grow and change **with the help of** solar energy.

생물은 태양 에너지의 도움으로 자라나고 변화합니다.

• with the help of ~의 도움을 받아서

2 **Without** energy from the sun, no life would exist.

태양으로부터 얻는 에너지가 없다면, 그 어떤 생물도 존재하지 않을 것입니다.

• without ~ 없이

3 Plants use sunlight, carbon dioxide, minerals, and water to make their own food.

식물은 빛과 이산화탄소, 무기물, 그리고 물을 이용해서 스스로 먹이를 만들어 냅니다.

4 Animals usually eat other living things **to get** energy to live.

동물은 보통, 살기 위한 에너지를 얻기 위해 다른 생물을 먹습니다.

• to 부정사 : ~하기 위해

단어 받아쓰기

오디오에서 불러주는 단어를 받아쓰고 우리말 뜻을 쓰세요.

🎧 ED3-003

단어 쓰기   뜻 쓰기

①

②

③

④

⑤

⑥

⑦

⑧

⑨

⑩

1단계 느린 속도로 듣고 받아쓰기

🎧 ED3-004

1 _____ usually eat other living things to get _____ to _____.

2 _____ use sunlight, carbon dioxide, _____, and water to make their own _____.

3 _____ energy from the sun, no life would _____.

4 _____ things grow and change with the help of _____ energy.

2단계 정상 속도로 듣고 받아쓰기

🎧 ED3-005

1 _____ use _____, carbon dioxide, _____, and water to make their _____.

2 _____ things _____ and change with the help of _____ _____.

3 _____ eat other living things to get _____ to _____.

4 _____ energy from the _____, no _____ would _____.

1

Q: What do _____ _____ need to
_____?

A: They need _____, water, and _____
to _____.

2

Q: What do _____ _____ to make their
own _____?

A: Plants _____ _____, carbon dioxide,
_____, and water.

3

Q: Where do _____ _____?

A: Plants _____ where they get what they
_____ to _____.

4

Q: Why do animals _____ other _____
_____?

A: Because they do not _____ their
_____ _____ by themselves.

ED3-007~007R

Living Things

_____ and _____ are _____ things. _____ things _____ and _____ with the _____ of _____ energy. Without energy from the _____, no _____ would _____. Living things _____ _____, _____, and _____ to survive; they _____ _____.

_____ need _____, water, _____, _____, and _____ to grow. Plants _____ where they get what they need to _____, and they _____ new plants like _____. Plants use _____, carbon dioxide, _____, and _____ to _____ their own food. Animals usually _____ other _____ _____ (animals, plants, etc.) to get _____ to live. They do not _____ their _____ food by themselves.

Leaves, Stems, and Roots

＊ 식물의 잎, 줄기, 뿌리의 특징과 역할에 대한 표현을 듣고 받아써 봅니다.

핵심단어 따라 말하기

단어를 3회 들려줍니다. 한 번씩 듣고 따라 말해 보세요.

🎧 ED3-008

			1회	2회	3회
❶	**leaf** [liːf]	명 나뭇잎, 잎	✔		
❷	**stem** [stem]	명 줄기			
❸	**root** [ru(ː)t]	명 뿌리			
❹	**fix** [fiks]	동 고정시키다			
❺	**bury** [béri]	동 묻다			
❻	**fruit** [fruːt]	명 열매, 과일			
❼	**flat** [flæt]	형 편평한, 평평한			
❽	**provide** [prəváid]	동 제공하다			
❾	**nutrient** [njúːtriənt]	명 영양분			
❿	**soil** [sɔil]	명 토양			

핵심문장 따라 말하기

1회는 천천히 또박또박, 2·3회는 정상 속도로 따라 말해 보세요.

ED3-009

1회   2회   3회

① **Most** plants have leaves, stems, and roots.

대부분의 식물은 잎과 줄기, 그리고 뿌리를 가지고 있습니다.

• most 대부분의

② **With** sunlight and air, leaves make food.

잎은 햇빛과 공기를 이용해서 양분을 만듭니다.

• with ~를 가지고, ~와 함께

③ Food and water **move through** the stems to the other parts of the plant.

양분과 물은 줄기를 통해서 식물의 다른 부분으로 이동합니다.

• move through ~를 통해 이동하다

④ Roots **are** usually **buried** in the soil.

뿌리는 보통 흙 속에 묻혀 있습니다.

• be동사+과거분사 : ~되다, ~당하다(bury - buried - buried)

단어 받아쓰기

오디오에서 불러주는 단어를 받아쓰고 우리말 뜻을 쓰세요.

🎧 ED3-010

단어 쓰기　　　　　　　　　**뜻 쓰기**

1

2

3

4

5

6

7

8

9

10

1단계 느린 속도로 듣고 받아쓰기

ED3-011

❶ _____ are usually buried in the _____ .

❷ With _____ and air, _____ make food.

❸ _____ and water _____ through the _____ to the other parts of the plant.

❹ Most _____ have leaves, _____ , and roots.

2단계 정상 속도로 듣고 받아쓰기

ED3-012

❶ _____ and water _____ through the _____ to the other _____ of the _____ .

❷ Most _____ have leaves, _____ , and _____ .

❸ With _____ and air, _____ make _____ .

❹ _____ are usually _____ in the _____ .

1

Q: Why are _____ often _____?

A: It is because they need to _____ _____ in.

2

Q: What keeps the _____ in the _____?

A: _____ do that.

3

Q: What do _____ _____?

A: Roots _____ _____.

4

Q: What do most _____ _____?

A: Most plants have _____, _____, and _____.

Leaves, Stems, and Roots

Most plants have _____, _____, and _____. _____ are often _____, so they take _____ in. With _____ and _____, leaves make _____. _____ _____ leaves in the _____ and _____ a _____ for the plant to keep its _____ and _____. _____ and _____ _____ through the _____ to the other _____ of the plant.

_____ are usually _____ in the _____. They are not always _____ the _____, though. _____ do not have _____. They take _____ and _____, a sort of _____, from the _____. Roots also often _____ this _____. And they _____ the plants to the _____.

Flowers, Seeds, and Fruits

＊식물의 꽃, 씨, 열매의 특징과 역할에 대한 표현을
듣고 받아써 봅니다.

핵심단어 따라 말하기

단어를 3회 들려줍니다. 한 번씩 듣고 따라 말해 보세요.

🎧 ED3-015

1회　2회　3회

1 **colorful** [kʌ́lərfəl]　　형 화려한, 다채로운　　✓ ○ ○

2 **contain** [kəntéin]　　동 포함하다, 함유하다　　○ ○ ○

3 **produce** [prədʒúːs]　　동 생산하다　　○ ○ ○

4 **seed** [siːd]　　명 씨, 씨앗　　○ ○ ○

5 **carry** [kǽri]　　동 나르다, 이동시키다　　○ ○ ○

6 **natural** [nǽtʃərəl]　　형 천연의, 자연의　　○ ○ ○

7 **develop** [divéləp]　　동 성장하다, 발달하다　　○ ○ ○

8 **warmth** [wɔːrmθ]　　명 온기　　○ ○ ○

9 **ground** [graund]　　명 땅　　○ ○ ○

10 **break** [breik]　　동 부서지다　　○ ○ ○

핵심문장 따라 말하기

1회는 천천히 또박또박, 2·3회는 정상 속도로 따라 말해 보세요.

⌂ ED3-016

1회   2회   3회

1 A flower is a part of a plant.

꽃은 식물의 한 부분입니다.

2 Flowers contain the part **that** produces seeds.

꽃은 씨를 생산하는 부분을 포함합니다.

• that : ~하는 것

3 A seed is the part of a plant which can **grow into** a new plant.

씨는 새로운 식물로 성장할 수 있는 식물의 한 부분입니다.

• grow into 자라서 ~가 되다, ~로 성장하다

4 When the fruit **breaks apart**, the seeds can go into the ground and **begin to** grow.

열매가 쪼개지면, 씨는 땅속으로 들어가서 자라기 시작할 수 있습니다.

• break apart 부서지다, 쪼개지다   • begin to ~하기 시작하다

단어 받아쓰기

오디오에서 불러주는 단어를 받아쓰고 우리말 뜻을 쓰세요.

ED3-017

단어 쓰기   뜻 쓰기

1

2

3

4

5

6

7

8

9

10

1단계 느린 속도로 듣고 받아쓰기

🎧ED3-018

❶ A _____ is the part of a plant which can _____ into
a new _____ .

❷ _____ _____ the part that _____ seeds.

❸ When the _____ _____ apart, the seeds can go into
the _____ and begin to grow.

❹ A _____ is a part of a _____ .

2단계 정상 속도로 듣고 받아쓰기

🎧ED3-019

❶ A _____ is a _____ of a _____ .

❷ _____ _____ the part that _____ _____ .

❸ A _____ is the _____ of a plant which can _____
into a _____ _____ .

❹ When the _____ _____ apart, the _____ can go
into the _____ and begin to _____ .

ED3-020~020R

1

Q: What _____ the part that _____ _____?

A: A _____ _____ that part.

2

Q: Where can we _____ _____?

A: We can find seeds _____ _____.

3

Q: When do seeds _____ into the _____?

A: The _____ go into the _____ when _____ _____ apart.

4

Q: When do seeds need _____, _____, and _____?

A: They _____ them when they are _____ to _____.

24

Flowers, Seeds, and Fruits

A _____ is a part of a _____. In many _____,

the flower is its most _____ _____. Flowers

_____ the part that _____ _____.

A _____ is the part of a plant which can _____

into a _____ _____. When the _____ is ready

to _____, it needs _____, _____, and _____.

Seeds _____ the _____ that _____ the new _____

begin to _____. They are often _____ _____.

A fruit is the part of a plant that _____ its _____.

When the _____ _____ _____, the seeds can

_____ into the _____ and _____ to _____.

Most _____ we eat _____ a lot of _____ and

_____ _____.

Unit 04 All Kinds of Animals

* 포유류, 파충류, 양서류, 어류, 그리고 곤충의 특징에 대한
표현을 듣고 받아써 봅니다.

핵심단어 따라 말하기

단어를 3회 들려줍니다. 한 번씩 듣고 따라 말해 보세요.

🎧 ED3-022

1회 2회 3회

❶ **mammal** [mǽməl] 　　명 포유류　　✓ ○ ○

❷ **reptile** [réptail] 　　명 파충류　　○ ○ ○

❸ **amphibian** [æmfíbiən] 　　명 양서류　　○ ○ ○

❹ **creep** [kriːp] 　　동 기어가다　　○ ○ ○

❺ **beak** [biːk] 　　명 부리　　○ ○ ○

❻ **scale** [skeil] 　　명 비늘　　○ ○ ○

❼ **fin** [fin] 　　명 지느러미　　○ ○ ○

❽ **extinct** [ikstíŋkt] 　　형 멸종된　　○ ○ ○

❾ **gill** [gil] 　　명 아가미　　○ ○ ○

❿ **birth** [bəːrθ] 　　명 출산, 탄생　　○ ○ ○

핵심문장 따라 말하기

1회는 천천히 또박또박, 2·3회는 정상 속도로 따라 말해 보세요.

🎧 ED3-023

1회   2회   3회

1 **Mammals give birth to live young.**

포유류는 살아 있는 새끼를 낳습니다.

• give birth to ~을 낳다

2 **Reptiles creep.**

파충류는 기어 다닙니다.

3 **Amphibians are four-legged animals.**

양서류는 다리가 네 개 달린 동물입니다.

4 **Insects were the first animals capable of flight.**

곤충은 날 수 있는 최초의 동물이었습니다.

• capable of ~을 할 수 있는

단어 쓰기   뜻 쓰기

1

2

3

4

5

6

7

8

9

10

1단계 느린 속도로 듣고 받아쓰기

ED3-025

❶ Reptiles _____ .

❷ _____ give _____ to live young.

❸ _____ were the first animals capable of _____ .

❹ _____ are four-legged _____ .

2단계 정상 속도로 듣고 받아쓰기

ED3-026

❶ _____ were the first animals _____ of _____ .

❷ _____ are _____ _____ .

❸ _____ _____ to live _____ .

❹ _____ _____ .

대화문 받아쓰기

앞에서 배운 단어와 문장으로 이루어진 대화문을 듣고 받아써 보세요.

ED3-027~027R

1

Q: How do _____ _____?

A: They _____.

2

Q: How many _____ do _____ have?

A: They have _____ _____.

3

Q: What do _____ _____ their _____?

A: They _____ their young _____.

4

Q: What do _____ have for _____?

A: They have _____ for _____.

All Kinds of Animals

_____ give _____ to live _____. They _____ their young _____. Mammals can _____, _____, _____, or _____.

_____ lay _____. Their bodies are _____ with _____, and they have _____ to _____. Birds also have _____ with which they _____ _____.

_____ _____. They are _____, and most of them _____ _____. Many _____ groups of _____ are now _____.

_____ are _____ animals. They live in _____ and on _____ and lay _____ in _____. _____ live under _____. They have _____, _____ for swimming, and _____ for _____. _____ were the first animals _____ of _____. They _____ from _____.

What Animals Need to Live

＊ 동물이 살기 위해 필요한 다양한 요소에 대한 표현을
듣고 받아써 봅니다.

핵심단어 따라 말하기

단어를 3회 들려줍니다. 한 번씩 듣고 따라 말해 보세요.

🎧 ED3-029

| | | | 1회 | 2회 | 3회 |

① shelter [ʃéltər]   명 거주지, 서식지   ✔ ◯ ◯

② various [vɛ́(ː)əriəs]   형 다양한   ◯ ◯ ◯

③ protect [prətékt]   동 보호하다   ◯ ◯ ◯

④ necessary [nésəsèri]   형 필수적인, 필요한   ◯ ◯ ◯

⑤ sense [sens]   동 감지하다   명 감각   ◯ ◯ ◯

⑥ lung [lʌŋ]   명 폐   ◯ ◯ ◯

⑦ danger [déindʒər]   명 위험   ◯ ◯ ◯

⑧ avoid [əvɔ́id]   동 피하다   ◯ ◯ ◯

⑨ breathe [briːð]   동 숨 쉬다, 호흡하다   ◯ ◯ ◯

⑩ safe [seif]   형 안전한   ◯ ◯ ◯

핵심문장 따라 말하기

1회는 천천히 또박또박, 2·3회는 정상 속도로 따라 말해 보세요.

🎧 ED3-030

1회   2회   3회

① **Animals need food, water, air, and a safe place to live.**

동물들은 먹이와 물, 공기, 그리고 살 안전한 장소가 필요합니다.

• to 부정사 : ~하는, ~할

② **Animals have body parts to protect and help them.**

동물은 그들을 보호하고 도움을 주기 위한 신체 기관을 가지고 있습니다.

③ **Eyes and noses are used for finding food.**

눈과 코는 먹이를 찾는 데 사용됩니다.

• be used for ~에 사용되다

④ **Animals also have body parts that help them get air.**

또한 동물은 공기를 마시는 데 도움을 주는 신체 기관도 가지고 있습니다.

• help + 목적어 + 동사원형/to 부정사 : ~가 …하는 것을 돕다

Unit 05 33

단어 받아쓰기

오디오에서 불러주는 단어를 받아쓰고 우리말 뜻을 쓰세요.

🎧 ED3-031

단어 쓰기	뜻 쓰기
1	
2	
3	
4	
5	
6	
7	
8	
9	
10	

문장 받아쓰기

오디오를 듣고 빈칸에 알맞은 단어를 쓰세요.

1단계 느린 속도로 듣고 받아쓰기

ED3-032

❶ _____ have body parts to _____ and help them.

❷ Animals also have body parts that _____ them get _____ .

❸ Eyes and _____ are used for _____ food.

❹ Animals need _____ , water, air, and a _____ place to _____ .

2단계 정상 속도로 듣고 받아쓰기

ED3-033

❶ _____ and _____ are used for _____ .

❷ _____ have _____ parts to _____ and _____ them.

❸ Animals need _____ , water, _____ , and a _____ place to _____ .

❹ Animals also have _____ parts that _____ them _____ .

1

Q : What do animals use for _____ _____?

A : They _____ _____ and _____ for finding _____.

2

Q : Where do _____ _____?

A : Animals live _____ _____ or _____ _____.

3

Q : What can help animals _____ _____?

A : _____, wings, and _____ can help animals _____ _____.

4

Q : What is _____ for animals to _____ _____?

A : _____, _____, and _____ are necessary for them to _____ danger.

What Animals Need to Live

Animals _____ food, _____, _____, and
a _____ place to live. They _____ in _____ kinds
of _____. Some animals live _____ _____.
Others live _____ _____. A _____ is a _____
where animals can _____.

_____ have _____ parts to _____ and _____
them. _____ and _____ are used for _____
_____. Eyes, _____, and noses are also _____
for them to _____ _____. _____, _____, and
_____ can help them _____ _____.
Animals also have _____ parts that help them _____
_____. _____ are for _____ to _____ in water
while _____ are for other animals to _____ _____.

Unit 06 **What Animals Eat**

* 초식동물, 육식동물, 그리고 잡식동물의 먹이에 대한
표현을 듣고 받아써 봅니다.

핵심단어 따라 말하기

단어를 3회 들려줍니다. 한 번씩 듣고 따라 말해 보세요.

🎧 ED3-036

	1회	2회	3회

❶ shark [ʃɑːrk] 　명 상어 　✔ ◯ ◯

❷ omnivore [ámnivɔ̀ːr] 　명 잡식동물 　◯ ◯ ◯

❸ herbivore [hə́ːrbəvɔ̀ːr] 　명 초식동물 　◯ ◯ ◯

❹ grind [graind] 　동 갈다 　◯ ◯ ◯

❺ deer [diər] 　명 사슴 　◯ ◯ ◯

❻ adapt [ədǽpt] 　동 적응하다 　◯ ◯ ◯

❼ carnivore [kɑ́ːrnəvɔ̀ːr] 　명 육식동물 　◯ ◯ ◯

❽ rip [rip] 　동 뜯다 　◯ ◯ ◯

❾ tear [tɛər] 　동 찢다 　◯ ◯ ◯

❿ vegetable [védʒitəbl] 　명 채소 　◯ ◯ ◯

핵심문장 따라 말하기

1회는 천천히 또박또박, 2·3회는 정상 속도로 따라 말해 보세요.

🎧 ED3-037

1회   2회   3회

❶ They eat food to get energy.

그들은 에너지를 얻기 위해 먹이를 먹습니다.

• to 부정사 : ~하기 위해

❷ Herbivores such as horses, rabbits, deer, and elephants have teeth that adapted to grind vegetable tissues.

말, 토끼, 사슴, 그리고 코끼리와 같은 초식동물은 식물 조직을 갈 수 있는 데 적합한 이빨을 가지고 있습니다.

• that : ~하는 것

❸ Carnivores such as tigers, lions, and sharks have sharp teeth to rip and tear meat.

호랑이, 사자, 그리고 상어와 같은 육식동물은 날카로운 이빨로 고기를 뜯고 찢습니다.

• such as ~와 같은

❹ Humans are omnivores because they eat meat as well as vegetable matter.

인간은 채소뿐 아니라 고기도 먹기 때문에 잡식동물입니다.

• A as well as B B뿐만 아니라 A도

단어 쓰기

뜻 쓰기

1

2

3

4

5

6

7

8

9

10

문장 받아쓰기

오디오를 듣고 빈칸에 알맞은 단어를 쓰세요.

1단계 느린 속도로 듣고 받아쓰기

🎧 ED3-039

1 Humans are _____ because they eat _____ as well as _____ matter.

2 _____ such as tigers, lions, and sharks have sharp teeth to _____ and tear _____ .

3 _____ such as horses, rabbits, deer, and elephants have teeth that _____ to _____ vegetable tissues.

4 They eat _____ to get _____ .

2단계 정상 속도로 듣고 받아쓰기

🎧 ED3-040

1 They eat _____ to _____ .

2 _____ are _____ because they eat _____ as well as _____ matter.

3 _____ such as tigers, lions, and _____ have _____ teeth to _____ and tear _____ .

4 _____ such as horses, rabbits, _____ , and elephants have teeth that _____ to _____ tissues.

1

Q: Why do _____ have _____ _____?

A: Because they have to _____ and _____ _____.

2

Q: Whose teeth _____ to _____ _____ tissues?

A: The _____ of _____ adapted.

3

Q: What are people who mostly _____ _____ usually _____?

A: They are called _____.

4

Q: Are pigs and _____ _____?

A: No. They are _____.

What Animals Eat

Animals need _____ to _____. They _____

_____ to get _____. Some animals only _____

_____. They are _____. Herbivores such as

_____, rabbits, _____, and _____ have

_____ that _____ to _____ _____ tissues.

Some animals mostly _____ _____. They are

_____. Carnivores such as tigers, _____, and

_____ have _____ _____ to _____ and

_____ _____.

Some animals such as _____, bears, and _____ dogs

and _____ eat both _____ and _____ to _____

themselves with _____. They are _____.

_____ are omnivores because they eat _____ as

well as _____ matter. People who mostly _____

_____ are usually called _____.

Unit 07

Families and Changes

* 기술 발달에 따라 변화된 가정의 삶에 대한 표현을 듣고 받아써 봅니다.

핵심단어 따라 말하기

단어를 3회 들려줍니다. 한 번씩 듣고 따라 말해 보세요.

🎧 ED3-043

			1회	2회	3회
① **dirt** [dəːrt]	명 때, 먼지	✓	○	○
② **washboard** [wɑ́ʃbɔ̀ːrd]	명 빨래판	○	○	○
③ **clothes** [klouðz]	명 옷, 의류	○	○	○
④ **washing machine** [wɑ́ʃiŋ məʃiːn]	명 세탁기	○	○	○
⑤ **wash** [wɑʃ]	동 씻다, 세탁하다	○	○	○
⑥ **communicate** [kəmjúːnəkèit]	동 의사소통하다	○	○	○
⑦ **cellular phone** [séljələr foun]	명 휴대전화	○	○	○
⑧ **send** [send]	동 보내다, 전송하다	○	○	○
⑨ **social** [sóuʃəl]	형 사회적인	○	○	○
⑩ **touch** [tʌtʃ]	명 연락, 접촉	○	○	○

핵심문장 따라 말하기

1회는 천천히 또박또박, 2·3회는 정상 속도로 따라 말해 보세요.

🎧 ED3-044

1회   2회   3회

1 **A long time ago, families washed their clothes by hand.**

오래 전에는 가족이 손으로 빨래를 했습니다.

• by hand 손으로

2 **Times have changed.**

시대가 변했습니다.

• have + 과거분사 : ~해 왔다

3 **Families can wash more clothes in less time.**

가족은 더 적은 시간에 더 많은 옷을 세탁할 수 있습니다.

• can〈조동사〉+ 동사원형 : ~할 수 있다

4 **A long time ago, families wrote letters.**

오래 전에는 가족이 편지를 썼습니다.

단어 받아쓰기

오디오에서 불러주는 단어를 받아쓰고 우리말 뜻을 쓰세요.

🎧 ED3-045

단어 쓰기	뜻 쓰기

1

2

3

4

5

6

7

8

9

10

문장 받아쓰기

오디오를 듣고 빈칸에 알맞은 단어를 쓰세요.

1단계 느린 속도로 듣고 받아쓰기

ED3-046

❶ _____ have _____.

❷ A long time ago, families _____ their clothes by _____.

❸ A long _____ ago, families _____ _____.

❹ Families can _____ more _____ in _____ time.

2단계 정상 속도로 듣고 받아쓰기

ED3-047

❶ A _____ ago, families _____ _____.

❷ A long time ago, families _____ their _____ by _____.

❸ Families can _____ more _____ in _____.

❹ _____ _____.

① Q: What is good when we _____ a _____ _____?

A: We can wash _____ _____ in _____ time.

③ Q: A long time ago, how did families _____ their _____?

A: They _____ their _____ by _____.

③ Q: What do _____ _____ _____ do for us?

A: They _____ us _____.

④ Q: Today, how can we get in _____ with people who live _____ _____?

A: We can _____ on _____ _____.

ED3-049~049R

Families and Changes

A _____ time ago, _____ _____ their _____ by _____. They _____ _____ to get the _____ _____. This _____ a long _____. _____ have _____. Families still must _____ their _____, but most families _____ use _____. Families can _____ more _____ in _____ _____.

A long time ago, families did not have _____ to _____ in _____ with their _____ members who _____ _____ _____. They _____ _____. Today, we can _____ _____ the _____ or _____ _____ from _____, _____ phones, and tablet PCs to our family _____ who _____ _____ away. Facebook, Twitter, and other _____ _____ services also help us _____.

Changing Communities

＊ 과거와 현재의 교통수단과 여가생활을 비교하는 표현을
듣고 받아써 봅니다.

핵심단어 따라 말하기

단어를 3회 들려줍니다. 한 번씩 듣고 따라 말해 보세요.

🎧 ED3-050

| | | | 1회 | 2회 | 3회 |

1 community [kəmjúːnəti] 　명 지역사회, 공동체 　✔ ◯ ◯

2 streetcar [stríːtkɑ̀ːr] 　명 시내 전차, 전차 　◯ ◯ ◯

3 transportation [træ̀nspərtéiʃən] 　명 교통 　◯ ◯ ◯

4 lake [leik] 　명 호수 　◯ ◯ ◯

5 pond [pɑnd] 　명 연못 　◯ ◯ ◯

6 heated [híːtid] 　형 난방이 되는 　◯ ◯ ◯

7 pool [puːl] 　명 수영장 　◯ ◯ ◯

8 indoor [índɔ̀ːr] 　형 실내의 　◯ ◯ ◯

9 rink [riŋk] 　명 스케이트장 　◯ ◯ ◯

10 ride [raid] 　동 타다 　◯ ◯ ◯

핵심문장 따라 말하기

1회는 천천히 또박또박, 2·3회는 정상 속도로 따라 말해 보세요.

🎧 ED3-051

1회   2회   3회

1 **Years ago, many people rode streetcars pulled by horses.**

수년 전, 많은 사람들은 말이 끄는 시내 전차를 탔습니다.

• **streetcars pulled by** = streetcars which[that] were pulled by

2 **Today, most people use cars, buses, and subways for transportation.**

오늘날, 대부분의 사람들은 자동차와 버스, 그리고 지하철을 교통수단으로 이용합니다.

3 **Years ago, in the winter, people ice-skated outside on ponds and lakes.**

수년 전, 사람들은 겨울에 야외의 연못과 호수 위에서 스케이트를 탔습니다.

4 **Today, people can ice-skate all year long in indoor rinks.**

오늘날, 사람들은 일 년 내내 실내 스케이트장에서 스케이트를 탈 수 있습니다.

• **all year long** 일 년 내내

Step 1 단어 받아쓰기

오디오에서 불러주는 단어를 받아쓰고 우리말 뜻을 쓰세요.

🎧 ED3-052

단어 쓰기 | 뜻 쓰기

1
2
3
4
5
6
7
8
9
10

문장 받아쓰기

오디오를 듣고 빈칸에 알맞은 단어를 쓰세요.

1단계 느린 속도로 듣고 받아쓰기

🎧 ED3-053

❶ Today, people can ice-skate all year long in _____ rinks.

❷ Years ago, in the winter, people ice-skated _____ on ponds and _____ .

❸ Today, most people _____ cars, buses, and _____ for transportation.

❹ Years ago, many people _____ pulled by horses.

2단계 정상 속도로 듣고 받아쓰기

🎧 ED3-054

❶ Years ago, in the _____ , people ice-skated _____ on _____ and _____ .

❷ Years ago, many people _____ by _____ .

❸ _____ , most people _____ cars, buses, and _____ for _____ .

❹ Today, people can _____ all year long in _____ rinks.

1

Q: What is _____?

A: It is a _____ of _____ people or things from one _____ to another.

2

Q: _____, what do most people _____ for _____?

A: They _____ cars, _____, and _____.

3

Q: Today, where can _____ _____?

A: They can swim in _____ _____ all _____ long.

4

Q: Years _____, where did _____ _____?

A: They _____ in _____, ponds, and _____.

54

Changing Communities

Life in _____ has _____ over the _____. One of those _____ is in _____. Transportation is a _____ of _____ people or things from one _____ to another.

Years _____, many people _____ _____ _____ by _____. Today, most people _____ _____, buses, and _____ for _____.

Years ago, in the _____, people _____ _____ on _____ and _____. In the _____, they _____ in _____, _____, and oceans. _____, people can ice-skate all _____ long in _____ _____. People can still _____ in _____, _____, and _____. But they also can swim in _____ _____ all year _____.

Many Jobs

✻ 다양한 직업에 관한 표현을 듣고 받아써 봅니다.

핵심단어 따라 말하기

단어를 3회 들려줍니다. 한 번씩 듣고 따라 말해 보세요.

🎧 ED3-057

	1회	2회	3회

❶ earn [əːrn]   통 (돈을) 벌다   ✓

❷ job [dʒɑb]   명 직업

❸ office [ɔ́(ː)fis]   명 사무실

❹ pay [pei]   통 ~를 지불하다

❺ travel [trǽvəl]   통 여행하다, 이주하다 명 여행

❻ outdoors [àutdɔ́ːrz]   부 야외에서

❼ whole [houl]   형 전체의

❽ firefighter [fáiərfàitər]   명 소방관

❾ police officer [pəlíːs ɔ́(ː)fisər]   명 경찰관

❿ care [kɛər]   명 돌봄, 보살핌

핵심문장 따라 말하기

1회는 천천히 또박또박, 2·3회는 정상 속도로 따라 말해 보세요.

🎧 ED3-058

1회   2회   3회

① **To earn** means to get paid for the work you do.

돈을 번다는 것은 당신이 하는 일에 대한 대가를 받는다는 것을 의미합니다.

- to 부정사 : ~하는 것

② Some people travel **to do** their work.

어떤 사람들은 일을 하기 위해 여행을 하기도 합니다.

- to 부정사 : ~하기 위해

③ Some people help everyone in a community.

어떤 사람들은 지역사회의 모든 이에게 도움을 줍니다.

④ Today, many people work from home.

오늘날, 많은 사람들은 집에서 일을 합니다.

단어 쓰기

뜻 쓰기

1

2

3

4

5

6

7

8

9

10

문장 받아쓰기

오디오를 듣고 빈칸에 알맞은 단어를 쓰세요.

1단계 느린 속도로 듣고 받아쓰기

🎧 ED3-060

1 Today, many people _____ from _____.

2 Some people _____ to do their _____.

3 Some people _____ everyone in a _____.

4 To _____ means to get _____ for the work you do.

2단계 정상 속도로 듣고 받아쓰기

🎧 ED3-061

1 To _____ to _____ for the work you do.

2 Some people _____ in a _____.

3 Some _____ to _____ their _____.

4 _____, many _____ from _____.

ED3-062~062R

①

Q: _____, what can people who work from _____ work with?

A: They can _____ from home with _____.

②

Q: Can _____ be a _____ of work?

A: Yes, some people _____ to do their _____.

③

Q: Where does one _____ sometimes work to _____ _____?

A: One parent _____ _____ the home.

④

Q: When you _____ _____, what does that _____?

A: It _____ you _____ _____.

Many Jobs

Many _____ have _____. Most people _____ at their _____ to _____ _____. To earn _____ to _____ _____ for the _____ you do.

People _____ in many _____ _____, like _____ and _____. Some people _____ to do their _____. Some people _____ _____. Some people _____ everyone in a _____. _____ _____, teachers, bus drivers, and _____ help the _____ _____.

_____, many people _____ from _____. These people can do _____ _____ with _____ without _____ home.

Sometimes, one _____ works at _____ by taking _____ of the _____ and _____. Often, the other _____ works _____ the home to _____ _____.

Social Studies
Unit 10

Producers and Consumers

* 경제활동을 이끌어가는 생산자와 소비자에 관한 표현을 듣고 받아써 봅니다.

핵심단어 따라 말하기

단어를 3회 들려줍니다. 한 번씩 듣고 따라 말해 보세요.

🎧 ED3-064

| | | 1회 | 2회 | 3회 |

1 **producer** [prədʒúːsər] 　명 생산자 　✓ ○ ○

2 **consumer** [kənsjúːmər] 　명 소비자 　○ ○ ○

3 **goods** [gudz] 　명 제품, 상품 　○ ○ ○

4 **sell** [sel] 　동 판매하다, 팔다 　○ ○ ○

5 **grow** [grou] 　동 기르다, 재배하다 　○ ○ ○

6 **buy** [bai] 　동 사다, 구입하다 　○ ○ ○

7 **farmer** [fáːrmər] 　명 농부 　○ ○ ○

8 **market** [máːrkit] 　명 시장 　○ ○ ○

9 **reason** [ríːzən] 　명 이유 　○ ○ ○

10 **become** [bikʌ́m] 　동 ~가 되다 　○ ○ ○

62

핵심문장 따라 말하기

1회는 천천히 또박또박, 2·3회는 정상 속도로 따라 말해 보세요.

🎧 ED3-065

1회   2회   3회

1 **Producers make goods to sell.**

생산자는 물건을 만들어서 판매합니다.

• to 부정사 : ~하는, ~할

2 **When farmers grow apples to sell, they are producers.**

농부가 사과를 재배해서 판매할 때, 농부는 생산자입니다.

• when 〈접속사〉 : ~할 때

3 **Consumers eat or use things that are grown or made by producers.**

소비자는 생산자가 재배하거나 만든 것을 먹거나 사용합니다.

• that : ~하는 것

4 **We all have things that we need or want to buy.**

우리 모두에게는 필요하거나 사고 싶은 것이 있습니다.

• that : ~가 …하는 것

단어 받아쓰기

오디오에서 불러주는 단어를 받아쓰고 우리말 뜻을 쓰세요.

ED3-066

	단어 쓰기		뜻 쓰기
1			
2			
3			
4			
5			
6			
7			
8			
9			
10			

1단계 느린 속도로 듣고 받아쓰기

ED3-067

❶ When farmers _____ apples to sell, they are _____ .

❷ Producers make _____ to _____ .

❸ We all have things that we _____ or _____ to buy.

❹ _____ eat or _____ things that are grown or _____ by producers.

2단계 정상 속도로 듣고 받아쓰기

ED3-068

❶ _____ or _____ things that are _____ or _____ by producers.

❷ _____ make _____ to _____ .

❸ When _____ apples to _____ , they are _____ .

❹ We all _____ things that we _____ or _____ to _____ .

ED3-069~069R

1 Q: What do _____ _____?

A: Consumers _____ or _____ things that are _____ or _____ by _____.

2 Q: What do _____ _____?

A: They _____ goods to _____.

3 Q: What do we call farmers who _____ apples to _____?

A: We call them _____.

4 Q: When farmers _____ a cup at a _____, who are they?

A: They are _____.

Producers and Consumers

Producers _____ _____ to _____. People who _____
goods to _____ also can be called _____. When farmers
_____ _____ to _____, they are _____.
The farmers _____ their _____ to _____ or
_____. Then, people _____ the _____ there.
_____ eat or _____ things that are _____ or
_____ by _____.
_____ of us are _____. The _____ is that we
all have _____ and _____. We all have things that we
_____ or _____ to _____.
The farmers _____ apples to _____ are _____.
But, when they _____ a _____ at a _____, they
become _____.

Unit 11 Egypt

＊ 인류 문명의 4대 발상지 중 하나인 이집트에 관한 표현을
듣고 받아써 봅니다.

핵심단어 따라 말하기

단어를 3회 들려줍니다. 한 번씩 듣고 따라 말해 보세요.

🎧 ED3-071

1회 2회 3회

① **hunt** [hʌnt]   동 사냥하다 ✔ ○ ○

② **learn** [ləːrn]   동 배우다, 학습하다 ○ ○ ○

③ **grassland** [grǽslænd]   명 목초지 ○ ○ ○

④ **gather** [gǽðər]   동 모이다 ○ ○ ○

⑤ **cave** [keiv]   명 동굴 ○ ○ ○

⑥ **pharaoh** [férou]   명 파라오 ○ ○ ○

⑦ **wild** [waild]   형 야생의 ○ ○ ○

⑧ **lucky** [lʌ́ki]   형 운이 좋은, 행운의 ○ ○ ○

⑨ **village** [vílidʒ]   명 마을 ○ ○ ○

⑩ **feed** [fiːd]   동 먹이다, 부양하다 ○ ○ ○

핵심문장 따라 말하기

1회는 천천히 또박또박, 2·3회는 정상 속도로 따라 말해 보세요.

🎧 ED3-072

1회   2회   3회

❶ They **had to keep moving** from one grassland to another to feed themselves.

그들은 먹고살기 위해 한 목초지에서 또 다른 목초지로 계속 이동해야 했습니다.

• have/had to ~해야 한다/했다   • keep -ing 계속 ~하다

❷ When people planted food and gathered together into villages, they could sleep in the buildings they made **for themselves**.

사람들이 식량을 재배하고 마을에 모여 살면서, 그들은 스스로 지은 건물에서 잠을 잘 수 있었습니다.

• for oneself 스스로

❸ One country **where** people started growing crops and building houses was Egypt.

사람들이 작물을 재배하고 집을 짓기 시작했던 한 나라는 바로 이집트였습니다.

• where : ~하는 곳(= in which)

❹ King Tut lived in Egypt beside **the longest river in the world**, the Nile.

투트 왕은 세계에서 가장 긴 강인 나일 강 옆에 살았습니다.

• the + 최상급 + 단수명사 + in + 장소 : ~에서 가장 …한 것

단어 받아쓰기

오디오에서 불러주는 단어를 받아쓰고 우리말 뜻을 쓰세요.

🎧 ED3-073

단어 쓰기 | 뜻 쓰기

1

2

3

4

5

6

7

8

9

10

🎧 ED3-074

❶ They had to _____ _____ from one grassland to another to _____ themselves.

❷ One _____ where people started _____ crops and _____ houses was Egypt.

❸ When people planted food and _____ together into villages, they could _____ in the _____ they made for themselves.

❹ King Tut lived in Egypt beside the _____ in the world, the Nile.

🎧 ED3-075

❶ When people _____ food and _____ together into _____, they could _____ in the _____ they made for themselves.

❷ One _____ where people started _____ and _____ was Egypt.

❸ King Tut _____ in Egypt beside the _____ in the world, the _____.

❹ They had to _____ from one _____ to another to _____ themselves.

ED3-076~076R

❶ Q: In the _____ times, what did people do to _____ _____?

A: They had to _____ _____ from one _____ to another.

❷ Q: There was a _____ in _____. What was he _____?

A: He was _____ the _____.

❸ Q: Who was _____?

A: He was a _____ _____ who lived beside the _____.

❹ Q: In _____, what did people _____ doing?

A: They started _____ _____ and _____ _____.

Egypt

In the _____ times, people did _____ _____

how to _____ _____. Until they _____, they had

to _____ _____ _____. They had to _____

_____ from one _____ to another to _____

themselves. Sometimes they were _____ and could

_____ in _____.

When people _____ food and _____ together into

_____, they could _____ in the _____ they

_____ for themselves. One _____ where people started

_____ _____ and _____ _____ was Egypt.

There was a _____ in _____. This king was

_____ the _____. One _____ _____ was

_____ Tutankhamen, or _____ Tut, for _____.

He _____ in Egypt beside the _____ _____ in

the world, the _____.

The Nile

✳ 나일강의 지리적 특징과 나일강이 이집트 문명에 미친
영향에 대한 표현을 듣고 받아써 봅니다.

핵심단어 따라 말하기

단어를 3회 들려줍니다. 한 번씩 듣고 따라 말해 보세요.

🎧 ED3-078

| | | 1회 | 2회 | 3회 |

1 **desert** [dézərt]　　명 사막　　✓ ○ ○

2 **central** [séntrəl]　　형 중앙의　　○ ○ ○

3 **end** [end]　　동 끝나다　　○ ○ ○

4 **flood** [flʌd]　　명 범람 동 범람하다, 침수되다　　○ ○ ○

5 **bank** [bæŋk]　　명 둑, 제방　　○ ○ ○

6 **moist** [mɔist]　　형 촉촉한　　○ ○ ○

7 **depend** [dipénd]　　동 의존하다　　○ ○ ○

8 **overflow** [óuvərflòu]　　동 넘치다, 넘쳐흐르다　　○ ○ ○

9 **city** [síti]　　명 도시　　○ ○ ○

10 **pass** [pæs]　　동 통과하다, 지나가다　　○ ○ ○

핵심문장 따라 말하기

1회는 천천히 또박또박, 2·3회는 정상 속도로 따라 말해 보세요.

ED3-079

1회   2회   3회

① The Nile begins in Central Africa.

나일 강은 중앙 아프리카에서 시작됩니다.

② Everything in Ancient Egypt **depended on** the overflowing of the Nile.

고대 이집트의 모든 것은 나일 강의 범람에 의존했습니다.

• depend on ~에 의존하다, 기대다, 신뢰하다

③ The water left rich and moist soil on its banks for ten miles.

그 물은 강둑에 10마일에 걸쳐, 비옥하고 촉촉한 토양을 남겨 주었습니다.

④ **Being able to** grow crops in one place meant that the people no longer had to move around.

한 곳에서 작물을 재배할 수 있다는 것은 더 이상 옮겨 다니지 않아도 된다는 것을 의미했습니다.

• be able to ~할 수 있다

단어 받아쓰기

오디오에서 불러주는 단어를 받아쓰고 우리말 뜻을 쓰세요.

🎧 ED3-080

단어 쓰기   뜻 쓰기

1

2

3

4

5

6

7

8

9

10

1단계 느린 속도로 듣고 받아쓰기

🎧 ED3-081

❶ Everything in _____ Egypt _____ on the overflowing _____ of the _____.

❷ The Nile _____ in _____ Africa.

❸ The water left _____ and _____ soil on its banks for ten miles.

❹ Being _____ to grow _____ in one place meant that the people no longer had to _____ around.

2단계 정상 속도로 듣고 받아쓰기

🎧 ED3-082

❶ The Nile _____ in _____.

❷ The _____ left _____ and _____ on its _____ for ten miles.

❸ Everything in _____ Egypt _____ on the _____ of the _____.

❹ Being _____ to _____ in one place _____ that the people no longer had to _____ around.

1

Q: What did the _____ of the _____ _____ on its _____?

A: It left _____ and _____ _____ on its banks.

2

Q: In the _____ from the _____, what did farmers _____?

A: They _____ _____.

3

Q: Where does the _____ _____?

A: It begins in _____ _____.

4

Q: Where does the _____ _____?

A: It ends at the _____ _____.

The Nile

The _____ _____ in _____ _____.
It _____ through a great _____. It _____ at the
_____ Sea. Each year, the _____ part of
the _____ _____ over its _____. That was where
_____ _____.

Everything in _____ Egypt _____ on the _____
of the _____. The water left _____ and _____
_____ on its banks for ten miles. In the _____, the
_____ _____ _____.

Since it is very _____ in Egypt all year, the _____
could _____ a lot of _____. Being _____ to grow
_____ in one _____ _____ that the people no
longer had to _____ _____. They could _____
and _____ _____ and _____.

Unit 13 An Orchestra

* 관현악단의 특징과 지휘자의 역할에 대한 표현을 듣고 받아써 봅니다.

핵심단어 따라 말하기

단어를 3회 들려줍니다. 한 번씩 듣고 따라 말해 보세요.

🎧 ED3-085

	1회	2회	3회

1 orchestra [ɔ́:rkistrə] — 명 관현악단

2 percussion [pərkʌ́ʃən] — 명 타악기 (연주단)

3 string [striŋ] — 명 현악기 (연주단)

4 wind [wind] — 명 목관악기 (연주단)

5 brass [bræs] — 명 금관악기 (연주단)

6 conductor [kəndʌ́ktər] — 명 지휘자

7 respect [rispékt] — 명 존경

8 address [ədrés] — 동 호칭을 쓰다, 부르다

9 master [mǽstər] — 명 거장, 장인

10 musician [mju(:)zíʃən] — 명 음악가

핵심문장 따라 말하기

1회는 천천히 또박또박, 2·3회는 정상 속도로 따라 말해 보세요.

🎧ED3-086

1 The members of all the families of instruments come together in an orchestra.

관현악단에는 모든 악기군이 함께 모여 있습니다.

2 An orchestra has a conductor.

관현악단에는 지휘자가 있습니다.

3 The conductor **makes sure that** all the members of the orchestra play their best and do their job at the right time.

지휘자는 관현악단의 모든 단원들이 반드시 최고의 기량을 발휘하고, 제때 연주할 수 있도록 합니다.

• make sure that 반드시 ~하도록 하다

4 To show respect, people sometimes **address** the conductor **as** "maestro," which means "master."

존경을 표하는 의미에서, 때때로 사람들은 지휘자를 '마에스트로'라고 부르는데, 이 말은 '거장'이라는 뜻입니다.

• address A as B A를 B라고 부르다

단어 쓰기

뜻 쓰기

1

2

3

4

5

6

7

8

9

10

문장 받아쓰기

오디오를 듣고 빈칸에 알맞은 단어를 쓰세요.

ED3-088

1단계 느린 속도로 듣고 받아쓰기

1 An orchestra has a _____ .

2 The _____ makes sure that all the members of the _____ play their best and do their job at the right time.

3 To show _____ , people sometimes _____ the conductor as "maestro," which means " _____ ."

4 The members of all the families of _____ come _____ in an orchestra.

ED3-089

2단계 정상 속도로 듣고 받아쓰기

1 The _____ of all the families of _____ come _____ in an _____ .

2 An _____ has a _____ .

3 To show _____ , people sometimes _____ the _____ as "maestro," which means " _____ ."

4 The _____ makes _____ that all the members of the _____ their _____ and do their job at the right time.

1

Q: What _____ does a _____ play?

A: A conductor does _____ _____ an _____.

2

Q: What _____ come together in an _____?

A: _____, _____, _____, and _____ instruments.

3

Q: Who _____ _____ that all the members of the _____ _____ well?

A: The _____ does that.

4

Q: How does a conductor help the _____ in an _____?

A: A _____ helps them _____ together and _____ at the right time.

An Orchestra

The _____ of all the families of _____ –
_____, string, _____, and _____–come
_____ in an _____. It takes many _____
_____ many instruments to _____ up an _____.
An orchestra has a _____. The conductor does _____
_____ an _____. The _____ is a man or
woman who _____ in _____ of the orchestra and
helps the _____ _____ together and _____
when they are _____ to. The conductor is like the
_____ of a _____: he or she _____ _____
that all the members of the _____ _____ their
_____ and do their _____ at the right _____.
To _____ _____, people sometimes _____ the
_____ as "maestro," which means "_____."

Great Composers and a Symphony

* 교향곡의 특징 및 교향곡 작곡가들에 관한 표현을 듣고 받아써 봅니다.

핵심단어 따라 말하기

단어를 3회 들려줍니다. 한 번씩 듣고 따라 말해 보세요.

🎧 ED3-092

| | | 1회 | 2회 | 3회 |

1 classical [klǽsikəl]　　형 고전적인, 고전의　✓ ○ ○

2 symphony [símfəni]　　명 교향곡　○ ○ ○

3 composer [kəmpóuzər]　　명 작곡가　○ ○ ○

4 piece [piːs]　　명 작품, 조각　○ ○ ○

5 movement [múːvmənt]　　명 악장, 움직임　○ ○ ○

6 quite [kwait]　　부 꽤　○ ○ ○

7 divide [diváid]　　동 나누다　○ ○ ○

8 known [noun]　　형 알려진　○ ○ ○

9 special [spéʃəl]　　형 특별한　○ ○ ○

10 way [wei]　　명 방식　○ ○ ○

핵심문장 따라 말하기

1회는 천천히 또박또박, 2·3회는 정상 속도로 따라 말해 보세요.

🎧 ED3-093

1회   2회   3회

① A symphony is a very special kind of classical music.

교향곡은 매우 특별한 유형의 고전음악입니다.

② It is a piece of music written for an orchestra to play.

그것은 관현악단이 연주할 수 있도록 쓴 음악 작품입니다.

③ The beginning of Beethoven's *Fifth Symphony* is **one of the most famous movements in** all of classical music.

베토벤의 〈5번 교향곡〉 도입부는 모든 고전음악 중에서 가장 유명한 악장 중의 하나입니다.

• one of the + 최상급 + 복수명사 + in : ~에서 가장 …한 것 중 하나

④ Joseph Haydn **is known as** the "Father of the Symphony."

요제프 하이든은 '교향곡의 아버지'로 알려져 있습니다.

• be known as ~로 알려져 있다

단어 받아쓰기

오디오에서 불러주는 단어를 받아쓰고 우리말 뜻을 쓰세요.

🎧 ED3-094

단어 쓰기　　　　　　　**뜻 쓰기**

1

2

3

4

5

6

7

8

9

10

1단계 느린 속도로 듣고 받아쓰기

ED3-095

1 It is a piece of _____ written for an _____ to play.

2 A _____ is a very special kind of _____ music.

3 Joseph Haydn is known as the "_____ of the _____."

4 The _____ of Beethoven's *Fifth Symphony* is one of the most famous _____ in all of classical music.

2단계 정상 속도로 듣고 받아쓰기

ED3-096

1 Joseph Haydn is _____ as the "_____ of the _____."

2 A _____ is a very _____ of _____ music.

3 The _____ of Beethoven's *Fifth Symphony* is one of the most _____ in all of _____ music.

4 It is a _____ of _____ written for an _____ to _____.

ED3-097~097R

1

Q: Does it take long to _____ to an _____ _____?

A: Yes, a symphony is _____ a _____ _____ of _____.

2

Q: What is _____ by Mozart, Bach, and Beethoven _____?

A: Their music is called _____ _____.

3

Q: How _____ is the _____ of Beethoven's *Fifth Symphony*?

A: It is one of the most _____ _____ in all of _____ music.

4

Q: How many _____ did Mozart _____?

A: He wrote _____ _____.

Great Composers and a Symphony

Music by _____ such as Mozart, Bach, Beethoven, and Tchaikovsky is called _____ _____.

A _____ is a very _____ kind of _____ _____. It is a _____ of _____ written for an _____ to _____. It may be quite a _____ _____—sometimes half an hour or more. It is _____ into _____—usually 3 or 4 parts of them. They are _____ _____.

There are lots of different ways of _____ a _____. Mozart _____ forty-one _____. Beethoven wrote _____ great _____. The _____ of Beethoven's *Fifth Symphony* is one of the most _____ _____ in all of _____ _____. Joseph Haydn is _____ _____ the "_____ of the _____."

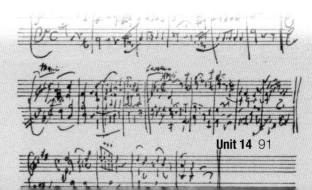

Unit 15 **Opera**

* 오페라의 특징을 듣고 받아써 봅니다.

핵심단어 따라 말하기

단어를 3회 들려줍니다. 한 번씩 듣고 따라 말해 보세요.

🎧 ED3-099

| | | 1회 | 2회 | 3회 |

1 **opera** [ɑ́:prə] 명 오페라

2 **play** [plei] 명 연극

3 **instead** [instéd] 부 대신에

4 **stage** [steidʒ] 명 무대

5 **costume** [kɑ́stjuːm] 명 의상, 복장

6 **composer** [kəmpóuzər] 명 작곡가

7 **perform** [pərfɔ́ːrm] 동 공연하다

8 **actor** [ǽktər] 명 배우

9 **language** [lǽŋgwidʒ] 명 언어

10 **line** [lain] 명 대사

핵심문장 따라 말하기

1회는 천천히 또박또박, 2·3회는 정상 속도로 따라 말해 보세요.

ED3-100

1회　　2회　　3회

1 An opera is like a play in which everything is sung **instead of** spoken.

오페라는 모든 것을 말 대신에 노래로 하는 연극과도 같습니다.

• instead of ~ 대신에

2 In an opera, the actors sing and act out the story on the stage, too, but they do not speak their lines.

마찬가지로, 오페라에서도 배우들이 무대에서 노래를 부르고 줄거리를 연기하지만, 그들은 대사를 말하지 않습니다.

3 **While** they sing, an orchestra plays music for them to sing along with.

그들이 노래하는 동안에, 관현악단이 그들이 음악에 맞춰 노래할 수 있도록 음악을 연주합니다.

• while〈접속사〉: ~하는 동안에

4 Many operas **were written by** composers who lived in European countries, such as Italy, Germany, and France.

많은 오페라가 이탈리아와 독일, 그리고 프랑스와 같은 유럽 국가에 살았던 작곡가들에 의해 쓰여졌습니다.

• be동사 + 과거분사 + by : ~에 의해 …되다 (write - wrote - written)

단어 받아쓰기

오디오에서 불러주는 단어를 받아쓰고 우리말 뜻을 쓰세요.

🎧 ED3-101

단어 쓰기　　　　　　　　　**뜻 쓰기**

1

2

3

4

5

6

7

8

9

10

ED3-102

1단계 느린 속도로 듣고 받아쓰기

❶ Many _____ were written by _____ who lived in _____ countries, such as Italy, Germany, and France.

❷ In an opera, the _____ _____ and act out the story on the stage, too, but they do not _____ their lines.

❸ An opera is like a _____ in which everything is _____ instead of _____ .

❹ While they _____ , an _____ plays _____ for them to sing along with.

2단계 정상 속도로 듣고 받아쓰기

ED3-103

❶ An _____ is like a _____ in which everything is _____ _____ of _____ .

❷ In an opera, the _____ _____ and _____ out the story on the _____ , too, but they do not _____ their lines.

❸ While they _____ , an _____ _____ music for them to _____ along with.

❹ Many _____ were written by _____ who lived in _____ _____ , such as Italy, _____ , and France.

1

Q: In an _____, who plays _____ while the _____ _____?

A: An _____ _____ music.

2

Q: In an _____, is everything _____?

A: Yes, everything is _____ _____ of _____.

3

Q: Why do many people _____ _____ even though they do _____ _____ them?

A: Because the _____ and _____ are so _____.

4

Q: Where were many _____ _____ from?

A: They were from _____ _____.

Opera

An _____ is like a _____ in which everything is _____ _____ of _____. In a _____, people put on _____ and then go _____ to _____ out a _____.

In an _____, the _____ _____ and _____ out the story on the _____, too, but they do _____ _____ their _____. And while they _____, an _____ _____ music for them to _____ along with. Operas are usually _____ in _____ _____.

Many operas were _____ by _____ who lived in _____ _____, such as _____, _____, and _____. That is why many operas are _____ in other _____ than _____. But because the _____ and _____ are so _____, many people _____ to _____ to operas even if they do not _____ all the _____.

Ballet

* 발레의 특징에 대한 표현을 듣고 받아써 봅니다.

핵심단어 따라 말하기

단어를 3회 들려줍니다. 한 번씩 듣고 따라 말해 보세요.

🎧 ED3-106

1회 2회 3회

1 **ballet** [bæléi] 　　명 발레　　✓ ◯ ◯

2 **training** [tréiniŋ] 　　명 훈련　　◯ ◯ ◯

3 **control** [kəntróul] 　　동 통제하다, 조절하다　　◯ ◯ ◯

4 **spin** [spin] 　　동 돌다, 회전하다　　◯ ◯ ◯

5 **leap** [liːp] 　　명 높이뛰기, 도약　　◯ ◯ ◯

6 **balance** [bæləns] 　　동 균형을 유지하다　　◯ ◯ ◯

7 **beauty** [bjúːti] 　　명 아름다움, 미인　　◯ ◯ ◯

8 **tip** [tip] 　　명 끝　　◯ ◯ ◯

9 **air** [ɛər] 　　명 공중, 허공　　◯ ◯ ◯

10 **practice** [præktis] 　　동 연습하다　　◯ ◯ ◯

핵심문장 따라 말하기

1회는 천천히 또박또박, 2·3회는 정상 속도로 따라 말해 보세요.

🎧 ED3-107

1회 2회 3회

1 **Ballet can tell a story.**

발레는 이야기를 전달할 수 있습니다.

• can〈조동사〉+동사원형: ~할 수 있다

2 **Instead, in many ballets, the dancers tell a story through the way they move.**

대신에, 많은 발레에서 무용수들은 움직임을 통해 이야기를 전달합니다.

• the way+주어+동사: ~가 …하는 방식, 방법

3 **Ballet dancers have to practice for years to learn all they need to know.**

발레 무용수들은 알아야 하는 모든 것을 배우기 위해 수 년 동안 연습해야 합니다.

• have to+동사원형: ~해야 한다

4 **Sometimes they make high leaps into the air.**

때때로 그들은 공중으로 높이 뛰어오르기도 합니다.

• into the air 공중으로

단어 받아쓰기

오디오에서 불러주는 단어를 받아쓰고 우리말 뜻을 쓰세요.

🎧 ED3-108

단어 쓰기　　　　　　　　뜻 쓰기

1

2

3

4

5

6

7

8

9

10

문장 받아쓰기

오디오를 듣고 빈칸에 알맞은 단어를 쓰세요.

1단계 느린 속도로 듣고 받아쓰기

🎧 ED3-109

❶ _____ can tell a _____ .

❷ Sometimes they make high _____ into the _____ .

❸ Ballet dancers have to _____ for years to _____ all they need to know.

❹ _____ , in many ballets, the _____ tell a story through the way they _____ .

2단계 정상 속도로 듣고 받아쓰기

🎧 ED3-110

❶ _____ can _____ a _____ .

❷ _____ , in many ballets, the _____ tell a _____ through the _____ they _____ .

❸ Ballet dancers have to _____ for years to _____ all they _____ to _____ .

❹ Sometimes they _____ _____ into the _____ .

1

Q: How do _____ _____ tell a _____?

A: They _____ a story through the _____ they _____.

2

Q: Is ballet a type of _____ or _____?

A: It is a _____ of _____.

3

Q: Why do ballet _____ have to work at _____ their _____?

A: Because sometimes they _____ _____ and around.

4

Q: Why do _____ dancers have to _____ at _____ themselves?

A: Because sometimes they _____ only on the _____ of their _____.

Ballet

Ballet is a _____ of _____. It is only done by _____ who have had _____ _____. _____ can _____ a _____. In a ballet, there is _____, often _____ by an _____, but no one _____ or _____. _____, in many ballets, the dancers _____ a _____ through the _____ they _____. Some ballets _____ _____ you may _____, like the story of _____ _____. _____ _____ have to _____ for years to _____ all they _____ to _____. They have to _____ very hard and have very _____ _____. They have to work at _____ themselves and _____ their _____. Sometimes they _____ only on the _____ of their _____. Sometimes they _____ around and _____. Sometimes they make _____ _____ into the _____.

Shapes

* 원, 사각형, 삼각형 등 다양한 모양의 도형에 대한 표현을
듣고 받아써 봅니다.

핵심단어 따라 말하기

단어를 3회 들려줍니다. 한 번씩 듣고 따라 말해 보세요.

🎧 ED3-113

| | | 1회 | 2회 | 3회 |

❶ **shape** [ʃeip]　　　　　명 모양, 형태　　✔ ○ ○

❷ **circle** [sə́:rkl]　　　　명 원, 동그라미　　○ ○ ○

❸ **square** [skwɛər]　　　명 정사각형　　○ ○ ○

❹ **triangle** [tráiæŋgl]　　명 삼각형, 세모　　○ ○ ○

❺ **rectangle** [réktæŋgl]　명 직사각형　　○ ○ ○

❻ **diamond** [dáiəmənd]　명 마름모, 다이아몬드　　○ ○ ○

❼ **oval** [óuvəl]　　　　　명 타원형　　○ ○ ○

❽ **join** [dʒɔin]　　　　　동 연결하다　　○ ○ ○

❾ **point** [pɔint]　　　　　명 꼭짓점　　○ ○ ○

❿ **rest** [rest]　　　　　　동 정지해 있다, 쉬다　　○ ○ ○

핵심문장 따라 말하기

1회는 천천히 또박또박, 2·3회는 정상 속도로 따라 말해 보세요.

🎧 ED3-114

1회 2회 3회

① **When** lines join together, they make shapes.

몇 개의 선이 만나면, 도형을 만듭니다.

• when 〈접속사〉: ~하면, ~할 때에

② Circles roll and **make you think** of wheels, marbles, and balls.

원은 굴러가기 때문에 바퀴와 구슬, 공을 생각나게 합니다.

• make + 목적어 + 동사원형 : ~가 …하게 만들다

③ Squares and rectangles **seem to** rest in one place and make you think of big rectangular objects, like refrigerators.

정사각형과 직사각형은 한 곳에 정지해 있는 것처럼 보이기 때문에, 여러분이 냉장고와 같은 큰 직사각형을 떠올리도록 합니다.

• seem to ~하는 것처럼 보이다

④ Triangles have points, and the points can make you think of something moving in a certain direction, like **a rocket rising** into the sky.

삼각형은 꼭짓점이 있어서, 그 꼭짓점은 여러분으로 하여금 하늘로 날아오르는 로켓처럼 특정한 방향으로 움직이는 것을 떠올리게 할 수 있습니다.

• **a rocket rising** = a rocket which [that] is rising

단어 쓰기   뜻 쓰기

1

2

3

4

5

6

7

8

9

10

문장 받아쓰기

오디오를 듣고 빈칸에 알맞은 단어를 쓰세요.

1단계 느린 속도로 듣고 받아쓰기

🎧 ED3-116

1 _____ roll and make you think of _____, marbles, and balls.

2 _____ have _____, and the points can make you think of something moving in a certain direction, like a _____ rising into the sky.

3 _____ and _____ seem to _____ in one place and make you think of big rectangular objects, like refrigerators.

4 When _____ join together, they make _____.

2단계 정상 속도로 듣고 받아쓰기

🎧 ED3-117

1 When _____ together, they _____.

2 _____ and make you think of _____, _____, and balls.

3 _____ and _____ seem to _____ in one place and make you think of big _____ objects, like _____.

4 _____ have _____, and the points can make you think of something _____ in a certain direction, like a _____ into the sky.

1

Q: What can _____ you _____ of _____?

A: _____ and _____.

2

Q: What can make you think of _____, _____, and _____?

A: A _____.

3

Q: What can different _____ make you _____ and _____?

A: They can _____ us feel and think _____ things.

4

Q: What do _____ _____ from?

A: They _____ _____ _____.

Shapes

When _____ _____ together, they make _____.

Here are _____ _____: a _____, a _____,

and a _____. Here are three _____ _____: a

_____, an _____, and a _____.

Different _____ can sometimes make you _____

and _____ _____ things. _____ again at the

_____ and the _____. Which one makes you think

of _____ _____? _____ _____ and can

make you think of _____, _____, and _____.

_____ and _____ _____ to _____ in

one place and can make you think of big _____

_____, like _____. _____ have _____,

and the point can make you think of something _____

in a certain _____, like a _____ _____ into the

_____.

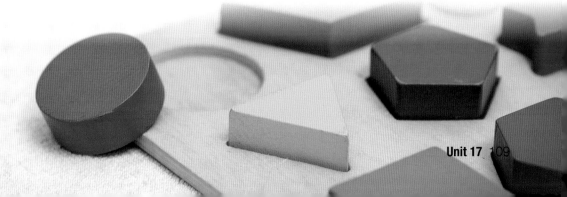

Portraits

※ 초상화의 정의와 가장 유명한 초상화 〈모나리자〉에
관한 표현을 듣고 받아써 봅니다.

핵심단어 따라 말하기

단어를 3회 들려줍니다. 한 번씩 듣고 따라 말해 보세요.

🎧 ED3-120

| | 1회 | 2회 | 3회 |

1 **portrait** [pɔ́ːrtrət] 　　　　명 초상화 ✓

2 **shelf** [ʃelf] 　　　　명 선반

3 **picture** [píktʃər] 　　　　명 사진, 그림

4 **draw** [drɔː] 　　　　동 (선으로) 그리다

5 **paint** [peint] 　　　　동 (색을 칠해) 그리다

6 **expression** [ikspréʃən] 　　　　명 표현, 표정

7 **face** [feis] 　　　　명 얼굴

8 **fascinate** [fǽsənèit] 　　　　동 마음을 빼앗다, 매료시키다

9 **Italian** [itǽljən] 　　　　형 이탈리아의　명 이탈리아인

10 **artist** [áːrtist] 　　　　명 예술가, 화가

핵심문장 따라 말하기

1회는 천천히 또박또박, 2·3회는 정상 속도로 따라 말해 보세요.

🎧 ED3-121

1회　2회　3회

1 A portrait is **what** we call a picture of a person.

초상화는 한 인물의 사진[그림]을 일컫는 것입니다.

• what : ~하는 것

2 Portraits **can be taken** with cameras, or they **can be drawn** or **painted**.

초상화는 사진으로 찍거나 그림으로 그릴 수도 있습니다.

• can + be동사 + 과거분사 : ~되어질 수 있다 (take - took - taken / draw - drew - drawn)

3 Perhaps **the most famous portrait in the world** is *The Mona Lisa*.

세상에서 가장 유명한 초상화는 아마도 〈모나리자〉일 것입니다.

• the + 최상급 + 단수명사 + in : ~에서 가장 …한 것

4 Portraits can tell a lot about a person and the time in which he or she lived.

초상화는 한 사람과 그가 살았던 시대에 대해 많은 것을 말해 줄 수 있습니다.

단어 받아쓰기

오디오에서 불러주는 단어를 받아쓰고 우리말 뜻을 쓰세요.

🎧 ED3-122

단어 쓰기   뜻 쓰기

1

2

3

4

5

6

7

8

9

10

문장 받아쓰기

오디오를 듣고 빈칸에 알맞은 단어를 쓰세요.

1단계 느린 속도로 듣고 받아쓰기

❶ _____ can tell a lot about a _____ and the time in which he or she lived.

❷ A _____ is what we call a _____ of a person.

❸ Perhaps the most _____ portrait in the world is *The* _____ _____ .

❹ Portraits can be _____ with cameras, or they can be drawn or _____ .

2단계 정상 속도로 듣고 받아쓰기

❶ Portraits can be _____ with _____ , or they can be _____ or _____ .

❷ _____ can _____ a lot about a _____ and the _____ in which he or she _____ .

❸ A _____ is what we call a _____ of a _____ .

❹ Perhaps the most _____ in the _____ is *The* _____ _____ .

① Q: Who _____ *The* _____ _____?

A: The _____ _____ Leonardo da Vinci _____ *The Mona Lisa*.

② Q: What has _____ people about *The Mona Lisa* for a _____ _____?

A: The _____ on *The Mona Lisa's* _____.

③ Q: What do you _____ a _____ of you on the _____?

A: We _____ it a _____.

④ Q: Can _____ be _____?

A: Yes, and they also can be _____ or _____ with _____.

Portraits

Have you had your _____ _____ at _____? Or is there a _____ of you on a _____ or _____ at home? That's your _____. That's what we _____ a _____ of a _____. _____ can be _____ with _____, or they can be _____ or _____. Perhaps the most _____ _____ in the world is *The* _____ _____. It was _____ by the _____ _____ Leonardo da Vinci about _____ _____ years ago.

_____ at the _____ on *The Mona Lisa's* _____. For hundreds of years, people have been _____ by her _____. What do you _____ she might be _____? Portraits can _____ a lot about a _____ and the _____ in which he or she _____.

Leonardo da Vinci,
The Mona Lisa (1503-1505)

Unit 18 115

Self-Portraits

* 자화상의 정의 및 반 고흐와 노만 록웰이 그린 자화상에 관한
표현을 듣고 받아써 봅니다.

핵심단어 따라 말하기

단어를 3회 들려줍니다. 한 번씩 듣고 따라 말해 보세요.

🎧 ED3-127

			1회	2회	3회
❶	**self-portrait** [selfpɔ́:rtrət]	명 자화상	✔	○	○
❷	**photograph** [fóutəgræf]	명 사진	○	○	○
❸	**Dutch** [dʌtʃ]	형 네덜란드의 명 네덜란드인	○	○	○
❹	**calm** [kɑ:m]	형 차분한	○	○	○
❺	**worried** [wə́:rid]	형 근심스러운	○	○	○
❻	**triple** [trípl]	형 3배의, 셋으로 된	○	○	○
❼	**feeling** [fí:liŋ]	명 느낌	○	○	○
❽	**idea** [aidí(:)ə]	명 아이디어, 발상	○	○	○
❾	**show** [ʃou]	동 나타내다	○	○	○
❿	**painter** [péintər]	명 화가	○	○	○

핵심문장 따라 말하기

1회는 천천히 또박또박, 2·3회는 정상 속도로 따라 말해 보세요.

🎧 ED3-128

1회   2회   3회

1 Sometimes an artist paints a portrait of himself.

때때로 화가는 자신의 초상화를 그리기도 합니다.

2 A self-portrait **does not have to look like** a photograph.

자화상은 반드시 사진처럼 보일 필요는 없습니다.

• **do not have to** 반드시 ~해야 할 필요는 없다   • **look like** ~처럼 보이다

3 The Dutch painter Vincent van Gogh painted 37 self-portraits.

네덜란드의 화가 빈센트 반 고흐는 37점의 자화상을 그렸습니다.

4 You get a very different feeling from **a self-portrait painted** by American artist Norman Rockwell.

미국의 화가 노만 록웰이 그린 자화상을 보면, 매우 다른 느낌을 받습니다.

• **a self-portrait painted** = a self-portrait which [that] was painted

단어 받아쓰기

오디오에서 불러주는 단어를 받아쓰고 우리말 뜻을 쓰세요.

ED3-129

단어 쓰기	뜻 쓰기
❶	
❷	
❸	
❹	
❺	
❻	
❼	
❽	
❾	
❿	

문장 받아쓰기

오디오를 듣고 빈칸에 알맞은 단어를 쓰세요.

1단계 느린 속도로 듣고 받아쓰기

ED3-130

❶ The _____ painter Vincent van Gogh painted 37 _____.

❷ You get a very _____ feeling from a self-portrait painted by American _____ Norman Rockwell.

❸ A _____ does not _____ look like a photograph.

❹ Sometimes an artist _____ a portrait of _____.

2단계 정상 속도로 듣고 받아쓰기

ED3-130

❶ Sometimes an _____ a _____ of _____.

❷ A _____ does not _____ look _____ a _____.

❸ The _____ painter Vincent van Gogh _____ 37 _____.

❹ You get a very _____ from a self-portrait painted by _____ Norman Rockwell.

1

Q: Does each _____ of a person _____ something _____?

A: Yes, it says something _____ about the _____ he _____ about himself.

2

Q: Should I paint myself the _____ _____ as _____?

A: No. You can _____ yourself in _____ _____.

3

Q: In _____ *Self-Portrait*, how many _____ did Norman Rockwell _____?

A: _____ _____.

4

Q: Did van _____ paint himself _____?

A: Yes, he _____ _____ self-portraits.

120

Self-Portraits

Sometimes an _____ paints a _____ of _____.

This is _____ a _____. A self-portrait does not have

to _____ _____ a _____. You can _____

yourself in many _____ _____, and each way will

_____ something _____ about the _____ you

_____ about yourself.

The _____ _____ Vincent van Gogh _____

_____ _____. This one, called _____,

_____ him when he was _____ _____ old.

How does van Gogh _____ to you? Does he _____

_____ or _____?

You get a very _____ _____

from a _____ _____ by

_____ _____ Norman Rockwell.

In this painting, called _____ *Self-*

Portrait, Rockwell has _____ with

the _____ of painting a picture of

_____. How _____ times does

Rockwell _____ _____ here?

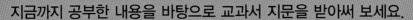

Vincent van Gogh,
Self-portrait (1889)

Unit 19 121

Still Lifes

* 정물화의 정의 및 정물화를 그리는 과정에 관한 표현을
듣고 받아써 봅니다.

핵심단어 따라 말하기

단어를 3회 들려줍니다. 한 번씩 듣고 따라 말해 보세요.

ED3-134

		1회	2회	3회

❶ **still life** [stil laif]　　　　　명 정물, 정물화

❷ **popular** [pápjələr]　　　　　형 인기 있는

❸ **china** [tʃáinə]　　　　　명 도자기

❹ **fine art** [fain ɑːrt]　　　　　명 예술

❺ **furniture** [fə́ːrnitʃər]　　　　　명 가구

❻ **arrange** [əréinʤ]　　　　　동 배치하다, 정렬하다

❼ **include** [inklúːd]　　　　　동 포함하다

❽ **raise** [reiz]　　　　　동 올리다, 인상하다

❾ **object** [ábdʒekt]　　　　　명 물체, 물건

❿ **texture** [tékstʃər]　　　　　명 질감, 결

핵심문장 따라 말하기

1회는 천천히 또박또박, 2·3회는 정상 속도로 따라 말해 보세요.

🎧 ED3-135

1회 2회 3회

① It **is called** a still life because the objects in the painting do not move.

그림 속의 물체가 움직이지 않기 때문에 정물화라고 불립니다.

• be called ~라고 불리다

② People **are not included** in a still life.

사람은 정물화에 포함되지 않습니다.

• be동사＋not＋과거분사 : ~되지 않다

③ To paint a still life, an artist first has to decide what objects to paint.

정물화를 그리기 위해서 화가는 먼저 어떤 물체를 그릴 것인지 결정해야 합니다.

④ **Once** the artist knows what to paint, he or she **has to** decide how to arrange the objects.

일단 화가가 무엇을 그릴지 안다면, 그는 물체를 어떻게 배치할 것인지 결정해야 합니다.

• once＋주어＋동사 : 일단 ~하면, ~하자마자 • have / has to＋동사원형 : ~해야 한다

Step 1

단어 받아쓰기

오디오에서 불러주는 단어를 받아쓰고 우리말 뜻을 쓰세요.

ED3-136

단어 쓰기 | 뜻 쓰기

1

2

3

4

5

6

7

8

9

10

124

1단계 느린 속도로 듣고 받아쓰기

ED3-137

❶ People are not _____ in a _____ _____.

❷ It is called a still life because the _____ in the painting do not _____.

❸ _____ the artist knows what to paint, he or she has to decide how to _____ the objects.

❹ To _____ a still life, an _____ first has to _____ what objects to paint.

2단계 정상 속도로 듣고 받아쓰기

ED3-138

❶ To _____ a _____, an artist first has to _____ what _____ to paint.

❷ _____ the _____ what to paint, he or she has to _____ how to _____ the objects.

❸ _____ are not _____ in a _____.

❹ It is _____ a still life because the _____ in the _____ do not _____.

1

Q: Where does the term _____ _____ _____ from?

A: It comes from the _____ that the _____ in the painting do not _____.

2

Q: Since when has _____ painting been _____?

A: It has been popular _____ the _____ _____.

3

Q: Who _____ still-life painting to a _____ _____?

A: _____ _____.

4

Q: How many people can we _____ in a _____ _____?

A: _____ are _____ _____ in a still life.

126

Still Lifes

There is a kind of _____ called a _____ _____. It is _____ a still life because the _____ in the painting do not _____. _____ are _____ _____ in a still life. _____ painting has been _____ since the _____ _____, when _____ painters _____ it to a _____ _____.

To _____ a still life, an _____ first has to _____ what _____ to paint. _____ _____ often _____ flowers, _____, books, _____, silverware, _____, or other small _____. Once the artist _____ what to _____, he or she has to _____ how to _____ the _____. What _____ and _____ will go _____ to one another? Where will the _____ _____? Will the still life _____ _____ with several different _____?

최신 개정 미국교과서로 독해 실력을 쑥쑥!

미국교과서 READING 시리즈!

미국교과서 READING Early 1	미국교과서 READING Starter 1	미국교과서 READING EASY 1	미국교과서 READING BASIC	미국교과서 READING ADVANCED 1
유치~초등 초급	초등 초급	초등 중급	초등 고급	중등 이상

단계	Early (전 3권)	Starter (전 3권)	Easy (전 3권)	Basic (전 3권)	Advanced (전 3권)
대상	유치 ~ 초등 초급	초등 초급	초등 중급	초등 고급	중등
특징	기초 어휘와 패턴 문장으로 리딩 시작	흥미로운 주제로 픽션&논픽션을 골고루	교과서 지식과 독해 실력을 동시에 쌓기 (논픽션)		
난이도 word counting	30~40단어	40~60단어	60~80단어	90~120단어	130~180단어

교재 특징

- 최신 개정 미국교과서 커리큘럼 반영
- 학생들의 수준에 꼭 맞는 단계별 리딩 학습
- 지문을 완전히 소화하도록 하는 풍부한 문제풀이!
- 완벽하고 철저한 학습을 돕는 부가 학습 자료 제공!

영어 실력 수직 상승을 위한 미국교과서 듣기 & 받아쓰기 단계별 프로그램

Level
3

미국교과서
리스닝 with
DICTATION

정답 및 해석

길벗스쿨

Unit 01

Living Things

Step 1 단어 받아쓰기 p. 10

❶ solar — 태양의
❷ metabolism — 신진대사
❸ space — 공간, 우주
❹ own — 자기 자신의, 고유의
❺ exist — 존재하다
❻ energy — 에너지, 기운
❼ nutrient — 영양분; 영양이 되는
❽ survive — 살아남다, 견디다
❾ undergo — ~를 경험하다, 겪다
❿ mineral — 광물, 무기물

Step 2 문장 받아쓰기 p. 11

1단계 느린 속도로 듣고 받아쓰기

❶ Animals usually eat other living things to get energy to live.
❷ Plants use sunlight, carbon dioxide, minerals, and water to make their own food.
❸ Without energy from the sun, no life would exist.
❹ Living things grow and change with the help of solar energy.

2단계 정상 속도로 듣고 받아쓰기

❶ Plants use sunlight, carbon dioxide, minerals, and water to make their own food.
❷ Living things grow and change with the help of solar energy.
❸ Animals usually eat other living things to get energy to live.
❹ Without energy from the sun, no life would exist.

Step 3 대화문 받아쓰기 p. 12

❶ Q : What do living things need to survive?
   A : They need food, water, and air to survive.
❷ Q : What do plants use to make their own food?
   A : Plants use sunlight, carbon dioxide, minerals, and water.
❸ Q : Where do plants grow?
   A : Plants grow where they get what they need to survive.
❹ Q : Why do animals eat other living things?
   A : Because they do not make their own food by themselves.

＊ 대화문 받아쓰기 해석

❶ Q : 생물은 생존하기 위해서 무엇이 필요한가요?
   A : 그것들은 생존하기 위해서 먹이와 물, 그리고 공기를 필요로 합니다.
❷ Q : 식물은 스스로 먹이를 만들기 위해서 무엇을 이용하나요?
   A : 식물은 빛과 이산화탄소, 무기물, 그리고 물을 이용합니다.
❸ Q : 식물들은 어디에서 자라나요?
   A : 식물은 생존하기 위해 필요한 것을 구할 수 있는 곳에서 자랍니다.
❹ Q : 동물들은 왜 다른 생물들을 먹나요?
   A : 그것들은 스스로 먹이를 만들어 내지 못하기 때문입니다.

Step 4 교과서 받아쓰기 p. 13

Living Things

Plants and animals are living things. Living things grow and change with the help of solar energy. Without energy from the sun, no life would exist. Living things need food, water, and air to survive; they undergo metabolism.

Plants need air, water, nutrients, sunlight, and space to grow. Plants grow where they get what they need to survive, and they make new plants like themselves. Plants use sunlight, carbon dioxide, minerals, and water to make their own food.

Animals usually eat other living things (animals, plants, etc.) to get energy to live. They do not make their own food by themselves.

1

other parts of the plant.
❹ Most plants have leaves, stems, and roots.

* 지문 해석

생물

식물과 동물은 생물입니다. 생물은 태양 에너지의 도움으로 자라나고 변화합니다. 태양으로부터 얻는 에너지가 없다면, 그 어떤 생물도 존재하지 않을 것입니다. 생물은 생존하기 위해서 먹이와 물, 그리고 공기를 필요로 합니다.; 그들은 신진대사를 겪습니다.

식물이 자라기 위해서는 공기, 물, 영양분, 햇빛, 그리고 공간이 필요합니다. 식물은 생존하기 위해 필요한 것을 구할 수 있는 곳에서 성장하고, 자신과 닮은 새로운 식물을 만들어 냅니다. 식물은 빛과 이산화탄소, 무기물, 그리고 물을 이용해서 스스로 먹이를 만들어 냅니다.

동물은 보통, 살기 위한 에너지를 얻기 위해 다른 생물(동물, 식물 등)을 먹습니다. 동물은 스스로 먹이를 만들지 못합니다.

Unit 02

Leaves, Stems, and Roots

Step 1   단어 받아쓰기   p. 16

❶ root   뿌리
❷ flat   편평한, 평평한
❸ stem   줄기
❹ soil   토양
❺ provide   제공하다
❻ leaf   나뭇잎, 잎
❼ bury   묻다
❽ fix   고정시키다
❾ fruit   열매, 과일
❿ nutrient   영양분

Step 2   문장 받아쓰기   p. 17

1단계 느린 속도로 듣고 받아쓰기

❶ Roots are usually buried in the soil.
❷ With sunlight and air, leaves make food.
❸ Food and water move through the stems to the

2단계 정상 속도로 듣고 받아쓰기

❶ Food and water move through the stems to the other parts of the plant.
❷ Most plants have leaves, stems, and roots.
❸ With sunlight and air, leaves make food.
❹ Roots are usually buried in the soil.

Step 3   대화문 받아쓰기   p. 18

❶ Q : Why are leaves often flat?
   A : It is because they need to take light in.
❷ Q : What keeps the leaves in the light?
   A : Stems do that.
❸ Q : What do roots store?
   A : Roots store food.
❹ Q : What do most plants have?
   A : Most plants have leaves, stems, and roots.

* 대화문 받아쓰기 해석

❶ Q : 식물들은 왜 보통 편평한가요?
   A : 그것은 잎이 빛을 흡수해야 하기 때문입니다.
❷ Q : 무엇이 잎이 빛을 계속 받을 수 있게 하나요?
   A : 줄기가 그렇게 합니다.
❸ Q : 뿌리는 무엇을 저장하나요?
   A : 뿌리는 양분을 저장합니다.
❹ Q : 대부분의 식물은 무엇을 가지고 있나요?
   A : 대부분의 식물은 잎과 줄기, 그리고 뿌리를 가지고 있습니다.

Step 4   교과서 받아쓰기   p. 19

Leaves, Stems, and Roots

Most plants have leaves, stems, and roots.
Leaves are often flat, so they take light in. With sunlight and air, leaves make food.
Stems keep leaves in the light and provide a place for the plant to keep its flowers and fruits. Food and water move through the stems to the other

parts of the plant.

Roots are usually buried in the soil. They are not always under the soil, though. Roots do not have leaves. They take water and nutrients, a sort of food, from the soil. Roots also often store this food. And they fix the plants to the ground.

＊지문 해석

잎, 줄기, 그리고 뿌리

대부분의 식물은 잎과 줄기, 그리고 뿌리를 가지고 있습니다.

잎은 대개 편평해서 빛을 흡수합니다. 잎은 햇빛과 공기를 이용해서 양분을 만듭니다.

줄기는 잎이 계속 빛을 받을 수 있게 해주고, 식물이 꽃과 열매를 계속 유지할 수 있는 장소를 제공합니다. 양분과 물은 줄기를 통해서 식물의 다른 부분으로 이동합니다.

뿌리는 보통 흙 속에 묻혀 있습니다. 그러나 뿌리가 항상 흙 속에만 묻혀 있는 것은 아닙니다. 뿌리에는 잎이 없습니다. 뿌리는 토양으로부터 물과, 일종의 먹이라고 할 수 있는 영양분을 흡수합니다. 뿌리는 보통 이 양분을 저장합니다. 그리고 뿌리는 식물을 땅에 고정시킵니다.

Unit 03

Flowers, Seeds, and Fruits

Step 1 단어 받아쓰기 p. 22

❶ contain	포함하다, 함유하다
❷ carry	나르다, 이동시키다
❸ seed	씨, 씨앗
❹ warmth	온기
❺ ground	땅
❻ colorful	화려한, 다채로운
❼ produce	생산하다
❽ natural	천연의, 자연의
❾ develop	성장하다, 발달하다
❿ break	부서지다

Step 2 문장 받아쓰기 p. 23

1단계 느린 속도로 듣고 받아쓰기

❶ A seed is the part of a plant which can grow into a new plant.
❷ Flowers contain the part that produces seeds.
❸ When the fruit breaks apart, the seeds can go into the ground and begin to grow.
❹ A flower is a part of a plant.

2단계 정상 속도로 듣고 받아쓰기

❶ A flower is a part of a plant.
❷ Flowers contain the part that produces seeds.
❸ A seed is the part of a plant which can grow into a new plant.
❹ When the fruit breaks apart, the seeds can go into the ground and begin to grow.

Step 3 대화문 받아쓰기 p. 24

❶ Q : What contains the part that produces seeds?
   A : A flower contains that part.
❷ Q : Where can we find seeds?
   A : We can find seeds inside fruits.
❸ Q : When do seeds go into the ground?
   A : The seeds go into the ground when fruits break apart.
❹ Q : When do seeds need water, air, and warmth?
   A : They need them when they are ready to develop.

＊대화문 받아쓰기 해석

❶ Q : 무엇이 씨를 생산하는 부분을 포함하고 있나요?
   A : 꽃이 씨를 생산하는 부분을 포함합니다.
❷ Q : 우리는 어디에서 씨를 발견할 수 있나요?
   A : 우리는 열매 안쪽에서 씨를 발견할 수 있습니다.
❸ Q : 씨는 언제 땅속으로 들어가나요?
   A : 씨는 열매가 쪼개지면 땅속으로 들어갑니다.
❹ Q : 씨는 언제 물과, 공기, 그리고 온기를 필요로 하나요?
   A : 그것들은 싹을 틔울 준비가 되면 그것들을 필요로 합니다.

Flowers, Seeds, and Fruits

A flower is a part of a plant. In many plants, the flower is its most colorful part. Flowers contain the part that produces seeds.

A seed is the part of a plant which can grow into a new plant. When the seed is ready to develop, it needs water, air, and warmth. Seeds carry the food that helps the new plant begin to grow. They are often inside fruits.

A fruit is the part of a plant that contains its seeds. When the fruit breaks apart, the seeds can go into the ground and begin to grow. Most fruits we eat contain a lot of water and natural sugars.

＊지문 해석

꽃, 씨, 그리고 열매

꽃은 식물의 한 부분입니다. 많은 식물에서, 꽃은 가장 화려한 부분입니다. 꽃은 씨를 생산하는 부분을 포함합니다.

씨는 새로운 식물로 성장할 수 있는 식물의 한 부분입니다. 싹을 틔울 준비가 되면, 씨는 물과, 공기, 그리고 온기를 필요로 합니다. 씨는 새로운 식물이 성장을 시작하도록 돕는 영양분을 나릅니다. 씨는 보통 열매 안쪽에 들어있습니다.

열매는 씨를 포함하고 있는 식물의 한 부분입니다. 열매가 쪼개지면 씨는 땅속으로 들어가서 자라기 시작할 수 있습니다. 우리가 먹는 열매의 대부분은 많은 수분과 천연당을 함유하고 있습니다.

Unit 04

All Kinds of Animals

❶ reptile   파충류
❷ amphibian   양서류
❸ scale   비늘
❹ gill   아가미
❺ mammal   포유류
❻ beak   부리
❼ extinct   멸종된
❽ creep   기어가다
❾ fin   지느러미
❿ birth   출산, 탄생

1단계 ▶ 느린 속도로 듣고 받아쓰기

❶ Reptiles creep.
❷ Mammals give birth to live young.
❸ Insects were the first animals capable of flight.
❹ Amphibians are four-legged animals.

2단계 ▶ 정상 속도로 듣고 받아쓰기

❶ Insects were the first animals capable of flight.
❷ Amphibians are four-legged animals.
❸ Mammals give birth to live young.
❹ Reptiles creep.

❶ Q : How do reptiles move?
   A : They creep.
❷ Q : How many legs do amphibians have?
   A : They have four legs.
❸ Q : What do mammals feed their young?
   A : They feed their young milk.
❹ Q : What do fish have for breathing?
   A : They have gills for breathing.

＊대화문 받아쓰기 해석

❶ Q : 파충류는 어떻게 어떻게 움직이나요?
   A : 그것들은 기어 다닙니다.
❷ Q : 양서류는 다리가 몇 개인가요?
   A : 그것들은 다리가 네 개입니다.
❸ Q : 포유류는 그들의 새끼에게 무엇을 먹이나요?
   A : 그것들은 그들의 새끼에게 젖을 먹입니다.
❹ Q : 어류는 숨을 쉬기 위해 무엇을 가지고 있나요?
   A : 그들은 숨을 쉬기 위해 아가미를 가지고 있습니다.

All Kinds of Animals

Mammals give birth to live young. They feed their young milk. Mammals can hop, walk, swim, or fly.

Birds lay eggs. Their bodies are covered with feathers, and they have wings to fly. Birds also have beaks with which they eat food.

Reptiles creep. They are cold-blooded, and most of them lay eggs. Many important groups of reptiles are now extinct.

Amphibians are four-legged animals. They live in water and on land and lay eggs in water.

Fish live under water. They have scales, fins for swimming, and gills for breathing.

Insects were the first animals capable of flight. They develop from eggs.

* 지문 해석

모든 종류의 동물

포유류는 살아 있는 새끼를 낳습니다. 그들은 새끼에게 젖을 먹입니다. 포유류는 뛰거나, 걷거나, 헤엄을 치거나, 날 수 있습니다.

새는 알을 낳습니다. 새의 몸은 깃털로 덮여 있고, 날 수 있는 날개가 있습니다. 새는 또한 음식을 먹을 수 있는 부리를 가지고 있습니다.

파충류는 기어 다닙니다. 파충류는 냉혈동물이고 대부분은 알을 낳습니다. 중요한 파충류 집단은 현재 많이 멸종되었습니다.

양서류는 다리가 네 개 달린 동물입니다. 양서류는 물과 육지에 살고, 물속에 알을 낳습니다.

어류는 물속에 삽니다. 어류는 비늘과, 헤엄을 치기 위한 지느러미, 그리고 숨을 쉬기 위한 아가미를 가지고 있습니다.

곤충은 날 수 있는 최초의 동물이었습니다. 그들은 알에서부터 자랍니다.

Unit 05

What Animals Need to Live

❶ various　　다양한
❷ safe　　안전한
❸ avoid　　피하다
❹ shelter　　거주지, 서식지
❺ danger　　위험
❻ protect　　보호하다
❼ lung　　폐
❽ sense　　감지하다; 감각
❾ necessary　　필수적인, 필요한
❿ breathe　　숨 쉬다, 호흡하다

1단계 느린 속도로 듣고 받아쓰기

❶ Animals have body parts to protect and help them.
❷ Animals also have body parts that help them get air.
❸ Eyes and noses are used for finding food.
❹ Animals need food, water, air, and a safe place to live.

2단계 정상 속도로 듣고 받아쓰기

❶ Eyes and noses are used for finding food.
❷ Animals have body parts to protect and help them.
❸ Animals need food, water, air, and a safe place to live.
❹ Animals also have body parts that help them get air.

5

Step 3 대화문 받아쓰기 p. 36

❶ Q : What do animals use for finding food?
　A : They use eyes and noses for finding food.
❷ Q : Where do animals live?
　A : Animals live on land or in water.
❸ Q : What can help animals avoid danger?
　A : Legs, wings, and fins can help animals avoid danger.
❹ Q : What is necessary for animals to sense danger?
　A : Eyes, ears, and noses are necessary for them to sense danger.

* 대화문 받아쓰기 해석

❶ Q : 동물들은 먹이를 찾는 데 무엇을 사용합니까?
　A : 그것들은 먹이를 찾는 데 눈과 코를 사용합니다.
❷ Q : 동물들은 어디에서 사나요?
　A : 동물들은 땅 위에서 또는 물속에서 삽니다.
❸ Q : 동물들이 위험을 피하는 데 무엇이 도움을 줄 수 있나요?
　A : 다리와 날개, 그리고 지느러미가 동물들이 위험을 피하는 데 도움을 줄 수 있습니다.
❹ Q : 동물들이 위험을 감지하는 데 무엇이 필요한가요?
　A : 눈, 귀, 그리고 코가 그들이 위험을 감지하는 데 필요합니다.

Step 4 교과서 받아쓰기 p. 37

What Animals Need to Live
Animals need food, water, air, and a safe place to live. They live in various kinds of places. Some animals live on land. Others live in water. A shelter is a place where animals can live.
Animals have body parts to protect and help them. Eyes and noses are used for finding food. Eyes, ears, and noses are also necessary for them to sense danger. Legs, wings, and fins can help them avoid danger.
Animals also have body parts that help them get air. Gills are for fish to breathe in water while lungs are for other animals to breathe air.

* 지문 해석

동물이 살기 위해 필요한 것
동물은 먹이와 물, 공기, 그리고 살 안전한 장소가 필요합니다. 동물은 다양한 장소에서 삽니다. 어떤 동물은 땅 위에서 삽니다. 다른 동물은 물속에서 삽니다. 서식지는 동물이 살 수 있는 장소입니다.
동물은 그들을 보호하고 도움을 주기 위한 신체 기관을 가지고 있습니다. 눈과 코는 먹이를 찾는 데 사용됩니다. 눈, 귀, 그리고 코는 위험을 감지하는 데도 필요합니다. 다리와 날개, 그리고 지느러미는 위험을 피하는 데 도움을 줄 수 있습니다.
또한 동물은 공기를 마시는 데 도움을 주는 신체 기관도 가지고 있습니다. 공기를 마시기 위한 용도로 다른 동물에게는 폐가 있는 반면, 물속에서 숨을 쉬기 위해 물고기에게는 아가미가 있습니다.

Unit 06

What Animals Eat

Step 1 단어 받아쓰기 p. 40

❶ grind　　　　　갈다
❷ adapt　　　　　적응하다
❸ rip　　　　　　뜯다
❹ shark　　　　　상어
❺ tear　　　　　　찢다
❻ vegetable　　　채소
❼ omnivore　　　잡식동물
❽ carnivore　　　육식동물
❾ herbivore　　　초식동물
❿ deer　　　　　　사슴

Step 2 문장 받아쓰기 p. 41

1단계 느린 속도로 듣고 받아쓰기

❶ Humans are omnivores because they eat meat as well as vegetable matter.
❷ Carnivores such as tigers, lions, and sharks have sharp teeth to rip and tear meat.

❸ Herbivores such as horses, rabbits, deer, and elephants have teeth that adapted to grind vegetable tissues.

❹ They eat food to get energy.

2단계 정상 속도로 듣고 받아쓰기

❶ They eat food to get energy.

❷ Humans are omnivores because they eat meat as well as vegetable matter.

❸ Carnivores such as tigers, lions, and sharks have sharp teeth to rip and tear meat.

❹ Herbivores such as horses, rabbits, deer, and elephants have teeth that adapted to grind vegetable tissues.

Step 3 대화문 받아쓰기 p. 42

❶ Q : Why do carnivores have sharp teeth?
  A : Because they have to rip and tear meat.

❷ Q : Whose teeth adapted to grind vegetable tissues?
  A : The teeth of herbivores adapted.

❸ Q : What are people who mostly eat plants usually called?
  A : They are called vegetarians.

❹ Q : Are pigs and bears carnivores?
  A : No. They are omnivores.

* 대화문 받아쓰기 해석

❶ Q : 육식동물은 왜 날카로운 이빨을 가지고 있나요?
  A : 그것들은 고기를 뜯고 찢어야 하기 때문입니다.

❷ Q : 어떤 동물의 이가 식물 조직을 가는 데 적합한가요?
  A : 초식동물의 이가 적합합니다.

❸ Q : 주로 채식을 하는 사람을 무엇이라고 부르나요?
  A : 채식주의자라고 불립니다.

❹ Q : 돼지와 곰은 육식동물인가요?
  A : 아니요. 그것들은 잡식동물입니다.

Step 4 교과서 받아쓰기 p. 43

What Animals Eat

Animals need energy to live. They eat food to get energy. Some animals only eat plants. They are herbivores. Herbivores such as horses, rabbits, deer, and elephants have teeth that adapted to grind vegetable tissues.

Some animals mostly eat meat. They are carnivores. Carnivores such as tigers, lions, and sharks have sharp teeth to rip and tear meat.

Some animals such as pigs, bears, and domestic dogs and cats eat both plants and meat to supply themselves with nutrition. They are omnivores.

Humans are omnivores because they eat meat as well as vegetable matter. People who mostly eat plants are usually called vegetarians.

* 지문 해석

동물의 먹이

동물은 살기 위해 에너지가 필요합니다. 동물은 에너지를 얻기 위해 먹이를 먹습니다. 어떤 동물은 식물만 먹습니다. 그들은 초식동물입니다. 말, 토끼, 사슴, 그리고 코끼리와 같은 초식동물은 식물 조직을 갈 수 있는 데 적합한 이빨을 가지고 있습니다.

어떤 동물은 거의 육류만 먹습니다. 그들은 육식동물입니다. 호랑이, 사자, 그리고 상어와 같은 육식동물은 날카로운 이빨로 고기를 뜯고 찢습니다.

돼지, 곰, 그리고 집에서 키우는 개와 고양이 같은 동물은 영양분을 공급하기 위해 채식과 육식을 모두 합니다. 이들은 잡식동물입니다.

인간은 채소뿐 아니라 고기도 먹기 때문에 잡식동물입니다. 주로 채식을 하는 사람은 보통 채식주의자라고 합니다.

Unit 07

Families and Changes

Step 1 단어 받아쓰기 p. 46

❶ washboard   빨래판
❷ dirt   때, 먼지
❸ social   사회적인

④ touch   연락, 접촉
⑤ communicate   의사소통하다
⑥ send   보내다, 전송하다
⑦ clothes   옷, 의류
⑧ cellular phone   휴대전화
⑨ washing machine   세탁기
⑩ wash   씻다, 세탁하다

Step 2   문장 받아쓰기   p. 47

1단계 느린 속도로 듣고 받아쓰기

❶ Times have changed.
❷ A long time ago, families washed their clothes by hand.
❸ A long time ago, families wrote letters.
❹ Families can wash more clothes in less time.

2단계 정상 속도로 듣고 받아쓰기

❶ A long time ago, families wrote letters.
❷ A long time ago, families washed their clothes by hand.
❸ Families can wash more clothes in less time.
❹ Times have changed.

Step 3   대화문 받아쓰기   p. 48

❶ Q : What is good when we use a washing machine?
     A : We can wash more clothes in less time.
❷ Q : A long time ago, how did families wash their clothes?
     A : They washed their clothes by hand.
❸ Q : What do social networking services do for us?
     A : They help us communicate.
❹ Q : Today, how can we get in touch with people who live far away?
     A : We can talk on cellular phones.

✳ 대화문 받아쓰기 해석

❶ Q : 우리가 세탁기를 사용할 때 좋은 점은 무엇인가요?
     A : 우리는 더 적은 시간에 더 많은 옷을 빨 수 있습니다.
❷ Q : 오래 전에는 가족이 어떻게 빨래를 했나요?
     A : 그들은 손으로 빨래를 했습니다.
❸ Q : 소셜 네트워크 서비스는 우리를 위해 무엇을 해주나요?
     A : 그것들은 우리가 의사소통하는 것을 돕습니다.
❹ Q : 오늘날, 우리는 멀리 사는 사람들과 어떻게 연락을 하나요?
     A : 우리는 휴대전화로 이야기를 할 수 있습니다.

Step 4   교과서 받아쓰기   p. 49

Families and Changes

A long time ago, families washed their clothes by hand. They used washboards to get the dirt out. This took a long time. Times have changed. Families still must wash their clothes, but most families today use washing machines. Families can wash more clothes in less time.

A long time ago, families did not have telephones to get in touch with their family members who lived far away. They wrote letters. Today, we can talk on the telephone or send e-mail from computers, cellular phones, and tablet PCs to our family members who live far away. Facebook, Twitter, and other social networking services also help us communicate.

✳ 지문 해석

가족과 변화

오래 전에는 가족이 손으로 빨래를 했습니다. 그들은 때를 벗겨내기 위해 빨래판을 사용했습니다. 이런 방식은 시간이 오래 걸렸습니다. 시대가 변했습니다. 가족들은 여전히 자신들의 옷을 빨아야 하지만, 오늘날 대부분의 가족은 세탁기를 사용하지요. 가족은 더 적은 시간에 더 많은 옷을 빨 수 있게 된 것입니다.
오래 전, 가족들은 멀리 사는 가족들과 연락을 하기 위한 전화기가 없었습니다. 그들은 편지를 썼습니다. 오늘날, 우리는 멀리 사는 가족들에게 전화로 이야기를 하거나 컴퓨터와 휴대전화, 태블릿 PC로 전자메일을 보낼 수 있습니다. 페이스북, 트위터, 그리고 많은 소셜 네트워크 서비스 또한 우리가 의사소통하는 것을 돕습니다.

Unit 08

Changing Communities

Step 1 단어 받아쓰기 p. 52

❶ lake — 호수
❷ pool — 수영장
❸ indoor — 실내의
❹ community — 지역사회, 공동체
❺ ride — 타다
❻ pond — 연못
❼ rink — 스케이트장
❽ streetcar — 시내 전차, 전차
❾ transportation — 교통
❿ heated — 난방이 되는

Step 2 문장 받아쓰기 p. 53

1단계 느린 속도로 듣고 받아쓰기

❶ Today, people can ice-skate all year long in indoor rinks.
❷ Years ago, in the winter, people ice-skated outside on ponds and lakes.
❸ Today, most people use cars, buses, and subways for transportation.
❹ Years ago, many people rode streetcars pulled by horses.

2단계 정상 속도로 듣고 받아쓰기

❶ Years ago, in the winter, people ice-skated outside on ponds and lakes.
❷ Years ago, many people rode streetcars pulled by horses.
❸ Today, most people use cars, buses, and subways for transportation.
❹ Today, people can ice-skate all year long in indoor rinks.

Step 3 대화문 받아쓰기 p. 54

❶ Q : What is transportation?
  A : It is a way of moving people or things from one place to another.
❷ Q : Today, what do most people use for transportation?
  A : They use cars, buses, and subways.
❸ Q : Today, where can people swim?
  A : They can swim in heated pools all year long.
❹ Q : Years ago, where did people swim?
  A : They swam in lakes, ponds, and oceans.

＊ 대화문 받아쓰기 해석

❶ Q : 교통수단이란 무엇입니까?
  A : 그것은 사람이나 물건을 한 장소에서 다른 장소로 옮기는 것을 의미합니다.
❷ Q : 오늘날, 대부분의 사람들은 교통수단으로 무엇을 이용합니까?
  A : 사람들은 자동차와 버스, 그리고 지하철을 이용합니다.
❸ Q : 오늘날, 사람들은 어디에서 수영을 할 수 있습니까?
  A : 사람들은 일 년 내내 온수풀에서 수영을 할 수 있습니다.
❹ Q : 수년 전, 사람들은 어디에서 수영을 했나요?
  A : 사람들은 호수와 연못, 그리고 바다에서 수영을 했습니다.

Step 4 교과서 받아쓰기 p. 55

Changing Communities

Life in communities has changed over the years. One of those changes is in transportation. Transportation is a way of moving people or things from one place to another.

Years ago, many people rode streetcars pulled by horses. Today, most people use cars, buses, and subways for transportation.

Years ago, in the winter, people ice-skated outside on ponds and lakes. In the summer, they swam in lakes, ponds, and oceans. Today, people can ice-skate all year long in indoor rinks. People can still swim in lakes, ponds, and oceans. But they also can swim in heated pools all year long.

❸ Some people help everyone in a community.
❹ To earn means to get paid for the work you do.

❶ To earn means to get paid for the work you do.
❷ Some people help everyone in a community.
❸ Some people travel to do their work.
❹ Today, many people work from home.

Step 3 대화문 받아쓰기 p. 60

❶ Q: Today, what can people who work from home work with?
   A: They can work from home with computers.
❷ Q: Can travel be a way of work?
   A: Yes, some people travel to do their work.
❸ Q: Where does one parent sometimes work to earn money?
   A: One parent works outside the home.
❹ Q: When you get paid, what does that mean?
   A: It means you earn money.

＊ 대화문 받아쓰기 해석

❶ Q: 오늘날, 집에서 일하는 사람들은 무엇을 이용해서 일을 할 수 있습니까?
   A: 그들은 집에서 컴퓨터를 이용해서 업무를 할 수 있습니다.
❷ Q: 여행이 일의 한 방식이 될 수 있나요?
   A: 네, 어떤 사람들은 일을 하기 위해 여행을 하기도 합니다.
❸ Q: 때로 부모 중 한 사람이 돈을 벌기 위해 어디에서 일을 합니까?
   A: 부모 중 한 사람은 집 밖에서 일을 합니다.
❹ Q: 당신이 대가를 받는다는 것은 무엇을 의미하나요?
   A: 그것은 당신이 돈을 번다는 것을 의미합니다.

Step 4 교과서 받아쓰기 p. 61

Many Jobs

Many people have jobs. Most people work at their jobs to earn money. To earn means to get paid for the work you do.

People work in many different places, like offices and stores. Some people travel to do their work.

＊ 지문 해석

변화하는 지역사회

수년 동안 지역사회 내에서의 삶은 변화해 왔습니다. 그러한 변화 중 하나는 교통수단입니다. 교통수단이란 사람이나 물건을 한 장소에서 다른 장소로 옮기는 방식을 의미합니다.

수년 전, 많은 사람들은 말이 끄는 시내 전차를 탔습니다. 오늘날, 대부분의 사람들은 자동차와 버스, 그리고 지하철을 교통수단으로 이용합니다.

수년 전, 사람들은 겨울에 야외의 연못과 호수 위에서 스케이트를 탔습니다. 그들은 여름에는 호수와 연못, 그리고 바다에서 수영을 했습니다. 오늘날, 사람들은 일 년 내내 실내 스케이트장에서 스케이트를 탈 수 있습니다. 사람들은 여전히 호수와 연못, 그리고 바다에서 수영을 할 수 있죠. 하지만 그들은 또한 일 년 내내 온수(溫水)풀에서 수영을 할 수도 있습니다.

Unit 09

Many Jobs

Step 1 단어 받아쓰기 p. 58

❶ job — 직업
❷ pay — ~를 지불하다
❸ earn — (돈을) 벌다
❹ whole — 전체의
❺ travel — 여행하다, 이주하다
❻ office — 사무실
❼ outdoors — 야외에서
❽ police officer — 경찰관
❾ firefighter — 소방관
❿ care — 돌봄, 보살핌

Step 2 문장 받아쓰기 p. 59

❶ Today, many people work from home.
❷ Some people travel to do their work.

Some people work outdoors. Some people help everyone in a community. Police officers, teachers, bus drivers, and firefighters help the whole community.

Today, many people work from home. These people can do office work with computers without leaving home.

Sometimes, one parent works at home by taking care of the house and family. Often, the other parent works outside the home to earn money.

* 지문 해석

여러 가지 직업

많은 사람들은 직업을 가지고 있습니다. 사람들은 대부분 돈을 벌기 위해 일을 합니다. 돈을 번다는 것은 당신이 하는 일에 대한 대가를 받는다는 것을 의미하죠.

사람들은 사무실과 상점처럼 다양한 장소에서 일을 합니다. 어떤 사람들은 일을 하기 위해 여행을 하기도 합니다. 어떤 사람들은 야외에서 일을 하죠. 어떤 사람들은 지역사회의 모든 이에게 도움을 줍니다. 경찰관, 선생님, 버스 기사, 그리고 소방관은 지역사회 전체를 돕습니다.

오늘날, 많은 사람들은 집에서 일을 합니다. 이런 사람들은 집을 나가지 않고도 컴퓨터를 이용해서 업무를 할 수 있습니다.

때로 부모 중 한 사람이 집에서 집과 가족을 돌보는 일을 합니다. 보통, 부모 중 나머지 한 사람은 돈을 벌기 위해 집 밖에서 일을 합니다.

Unit 10

Producers and Consumers

| Step 1 | 단어 받아쓰기 | p. 64 |

① farmer — 농부
② producer — 생산자
③ sell — 판매하다, 팔다
④ buy — 사다, 구입하다
⑤ consumer — 소비자

⑥ become — ~가 되다
⑦ market — 시장
⑧ grow — 기르다, 재배하다
⑨ goods — 제품, 상품
⑩ reason — 이유

| Step 2 | 문장 받아쓰기 | p. 65 |

1단계 느린 속도로 듣고 받아쓰기

① When farmers grow apples to sell, they are producers.
② Producers make goods to sell.
③ We all have things that we need or want to buy.
④ Consumers eat or use things that are grown or made by producers.

2단계 정상 속도로 듣고 받아쓰기

① Consumers eat or use things that are grown or made by producers.
② Producers make goods to sell.
③ When farmers grow apples to sell, they are producers.
④ We all have things that we need or want to buy.

| Step 3 | 대화문 받아쓰기 | p. 66 |

① Q : What do consumers do?
   A : Consumers eat or use things that are grown or made by producers.
② Q : What do producers do?
   A : They make goods to sell.
③ Q : What do we call farmers who grow apples to sell?
   A : We call them producers.
④ Q : When farmers buy a cup at a store, who are they?
   A : They are consumers.

* 대화문 받아쓰기 해석

① Q : 소비자는 무엇을 합니까?
   A : 소비자는 생산자가 재배하거나 만든 것을 먹거나 사용합니다.

❷ Q : 생산자는 무엇을 합니까?
  A : 그들은 물건을 만들어서 판매합니다.
❸ Q : 우리는 사과를 재배해서 판매하는 농부를 무엇이라고 부르나요?
  A : 우리는 그들을 생산자라고 부릅니다.
❹ Q : 농부가 상점에서 컵 하나를 산다면, 그들은 무엇이 되나요?
  A : 그들은 소비자가 됩니다.

Step 4　교과서 받아쓰기　p. 67

Producers and Consumers

Producers make goods to sell. People who grow goods to sell also can be called producers. When farmers grow apples to sell, they are producers.
The farmers sell their goods to stores or markets. Then, people buy the goods there. Consumers eat or use things that are grown or made by producers. All of us are consumers. The reason is that we all have needs and wants. We all have things that we need or want to buy.
The farmers growing apples to sell are producers. But, when they buy a cup at a store, they become consumers.

＊지문 해석

생산자와 소비자

생산자는 물건을 만들어서 판매합니다. 팔기 위한 상품을 재배하는 사람도 생산자라고 부를 수 있습니다. 농부가 사과를 재배해서 판매하면 생산자가 되는 것이지요.
농부는 자신의 상품을 상점이나 시장에 팝니다. 그러면 사람들은 그곳에서 상품을 삽니다. 소비자는 생산자가 재배하거나 만든 것을 먹거나 사용합니다.
우리 모두는 소비자입니다. 그 이유는 우리 모두는 필요한 것과 원하는 것이 있기 때문입니다. 우리 모두에게는 필요하거나 사고 싶은 것이 있죠.
사과를 재배해 파는 농부는 생산자입니다. 하지만 그 농부들이 상점에서 컵 하나를 산다면, 그들은 소비자가 되는 것이지요.

Unit 11

Egypt

Step 1　단어 받아쓰기　p. 70

❶ learn　　배우다, 학습하다
❷ pharaoh　파라오
❸ village　　마을
❹ hunt　　　사냥하다
❺ feed　　　먹이다, 부양하다
❻ gather　　모이다
❼ wild　　　야생의
❽ grassland　목초지
❾ cave　　　동굴
❿ lucky　　　운이 좋은, 행운의

Step 2　문장 받아쓰기　p. 71

1단계 느린 속도로 듣고 받아쓰기

❶ They had to keep moving from one grassland to another to feed themselves.
❷ One country where people started growing crops and building houses was Egypt.
❸ When people planted food and gathered together into villages, they could sleep in the buildings they made for themselves.
❹ King Tut lived in Egypt beside the longest river in the world, the Nile.

2단계 정상 속도로 듣고 받아쓰기

❶ When people planted food and gathered together into villages, they could sleep in the buildings they made for themselves.
❷ One country where people started growing crops and building houses was Egypt.
❸ King Tut lived in Egypt beside the longest river in the world, the Nile.

❹ They had to keep moving from one grassland to another to feed themselves.

Step 3 　대화문 받아쓰기　　　　p. 72

❶ Q : In the earliest times, what did people do to feed themselves?
　　A : They had to keep moving from one grassland to another.
❷ Q : There was a king in Egypt. What was he called?
　　A : He was called the pharaoh.
❸ Q : Who was Tutankhamen?
　　A : He was a young pharaoh who lived beside the Nile.
❹ Q : In Egypt, what did people start doing?
　　A : They started growing crops and building houses.

＊ 대화문 받아쓰기 해석

❶ Q : 고대에, 사람들은 먹고살기 위해 무엇을 했습니까?
　　A : 그들은 한 목초지에서 또 다른 목초지로 계속 이동해야 했다.
❷ Q : 이집트에는 왕이 있었습니다. 그 왕은 무엇이라고 불렸습니까?
　　A : 그 왕은 파라오라고 불렸습니다.
❸ Q : 투탕카멘은 누구였나요?
　　A : 그는 나일 강 옆에서 산 젊은 파라오였습니다.
❹ Q : 이집트에서 사람들은 무엇을 하기 시작했나요?
　　A : 그들은 작물을 재배하고 집을 짓기 시작했습니다.

Step 4 　교과서 받아쓰기　　　　p. 73

Egypt

In the earliest times, people did not know how to grow food. Until they learned, they had to hunt wild animals. They had to keep moving from one grassland to another to feed themselves. Sometimes they were lucky and could sleep in caves.
When people planted food and gathered together into villages, they could sleep in the buildings they made for themselves. One country where people started growing crops and building houses was Egypt.
There was a king in Egypt. This king was called the pharaoh. One young pharaoh was called Tutankhamen, or King Tut, for short. He lived in Egypt beside the longest river in the world, the Nile.

＊ 지문 해석

이집트

고대에, 사람들은 식량을 재배하는 방법을 몰랐습니다. 그 방법을 배울 때까지 그들은 야생 동물을 사냥해야만 했습니다. 그들은 먹고살기 위해 한 목초지에서 또 다른 목초지로 계속 이동해야 했죠. 때로는 운이 좋아 동굴 안에서 잠을 잘 수 있었습니다.
사람들이 식량을 재배하고 마을에 모여 살면서, 그들은 스스로 지은 건물에서 잠을 잘 수 있었습니다. 사람들이 작물을 재배하고 집을 짓기 시작했던 한 나라는 바로 이집트였습니다.
이집트에는 왕이 있었습니다. 그 왕은 파라오라고 불렸습니다. 한 젊은 파라오는 투탕카멘, 줄여서 투트 왕으로 불렸지요. 그는 세계에서 가장 긴 강인 나일 강 옆에 살았습니다.

Unit 12

The Nile

Step 1 　단어 받아쓰기　　　　p. 76

❶ end　　　　　끝나다
❷ overflow　　　넘치다, 넘쳐흐르다
❸ central　　　　중앙의
❹ desert　　　　사막
❺ flood　　　　 범람; 범람하다, 침수되다
❻ city　　　　　도시
❼ depend　　　　의존하다
❽ moist　　　　 촉촉한
❾ bank　　　　　둑, 제방
❿ pass　　　　　통과하다, 지나가다

13

문장 받아쓰기   p. 77

1단계 느린 속도로 듣고 받아쓰기

❶ Everything in Ancient Egypt depended on the overflowing of the Nile.
❷ The Nile begins in Central Africa.
❸ The water left rich and moist soil on its banks for ten miles.
❹ Being able to grow crops in one place meant that the people no longer had to move around.

2단계 정상 속도로 듣고 받아쓰기

❶ The Nile begins in Central Africa.
❷ The water left rich and moist soil on its banks for ten miles.
❸ Everything in Ancient Egypt depended on the overflowing of the Nile.
❹ Being able to grow crops in one place meant that the people no longer had to move around.

Step 3   **대화문 받아쓰기**   p. 78

❶ Q : What did the overflowing of the Nile leave on its banks?
 A : It left rich and moist soil on its banks.
❷ Q : In the soil from the Nile, what did farmers plant?
 A : They planted crops.
❸ Q : Where does the Nile begin?
 A : It begins in Central Africa.
❹ Q : Where does the Nile end?
 A : It ends at the Mediterranean Sea.

＊ 대화문 받아쓰기 해석

❶ Q : 나일 강의 범람은 강둑에 무엇을 남겨 주었습니까?
 A : 그것은 강둑에 비옥하고 촉촉한 토양을 남겨 주었습니다.
❷ Q : 나일 강에서 온 토양에 농부들은 무엇을 심었습니까?
 A : 그들은 작물을 심었습니다.
❸ Q : 나일 강은 어디에서 시작됩니까?
 A : 그 강은 중앙 아프리카에서 시작됩니다.
❹ Q : 나일 강은 어디에서 끝이 납니까?
 A : 그 강은 지중해에서 끝이 납니다.

Step 4   **교과서 받아쓰기**   p. 79

The Nile
The Nile begins in Central Africa. It passes through a great desert. It ends at the Mediterranean Sea. Each year, the northern part of the Nile flooded over its banks. That was where Egypt began.
Everything in Ancient Egypt depended on the overflowing of the Nile. The water left rich and moist soil on its banks for ten miles. In the soil, the farmers planted crops.
Since it is very warm in Egypt all year, the Egyptians could grow a lot of food. Being able to grow crops in one place meant that the people no longer had to move around. They could stay and build villages and cities.

＊ 지문 해석

나일 강

나일 강은 중앙 아프리카에서 시작됩니다. 나일 강은 거대한 사막을 통과합니다. 그 강은 지중해에서 끝이 납니다. 매년, 나일 강의 북부가 범람했습니다. 그곳이 바로, 이집트가 시작된 곳입니다.
고대 이집트의 모든 것은 나일 강의 범람에 의존했습니다. 강물은 강둑에 10마일에 걸쳐, 비옥하고 촉촉한 토양을 남겨 주었습니다. 그 토양에서 농부들은 작물을 심었습니다.
이집트는 일 년 내내 따뜻하기 때문에 이집트인들은 많은 식량을 재배할 수 있었습니다. 한 곳에서 작물을 재배할 수 있다는 것은 더 이상 옮겨 다니지 않아도 된다는 것을 의미했습니다. 이집트인들은 한 곳에 머물면서 마을과 도시를 건설할 수 있었습니다.

Unit 13

An Orchestra

Step 1   **단어 받아쓰기**   p. 82

❶ conductor   지휘자

14

❷ orchestra   관현악단
❸ respect   존경
❹ musician   음악가
❺ string   현악기 (연주단)
❻ brass   금관악기 (연주단)
❼ wind   목관악기 (연주단)
❽ master   거장, 장인
❾ percussion   타악기 (연주단)
❿ address   호칭을 쓰다, 부르다

Step 2   문장 받아쓰기   p. 83

1단계 느린 속도로 듣고 받아쓰기

❶ An orchestra has a conductor.
❷ The conductor makes sure that all the members of the orchestra play their best and do their job at the right time.
❸ To show respect, people sometimes address the conductor as "maestro," which means "master."
❹ The members of all the families of instruments come together in an orchestra.

2단계 정상 속도로 듣고 받아쓰기

❶ The members of all the families of instruments come together in an orchestra.
❷ An orchestra has a conductor.
❸ To show respect, people sometimes address the conductor as "maestro," which means "master."
❹ The conductor makes sure that all the members of the orchestra play their best and do their job at the right time.

Step 3   대화문 받아쓰기   p. 84

❶ Q : What instrument does a conductor play?
   A : A conductor does not play an instrument.
❷ Q : What members come together in an orchestra?
   A : Percussion, string, wind, and brass instruments.

❸ Q : Who makes sure that all the members of the orchestra play well?
   A : The conductor does that.
❹ Q : How does a conductor help the musicians in an orchestra?
   A : A conductor helps them stay together and play at the right time.

✳ 대화문 받아쓰기 해석

❶ Q : 지휘자는 어떤 악기를 연주하나요?
   A : 지휘자는 악기를 연주하지 않습니다.
❷ Q : 관현악단에는 어떤 악기군이 함께 모여 있습니까?
   A : 타악기, 현악기, 목관악기, 금관악기입니다.
❸ Q : 누가 관현악단의 모든 단원들이 반드시 최고의 기량을 발휘하게 합니까?
   A : 지휘자가 그렇게 합니다.
❹ Q : 지휘자는 어떻게 관현악단의 단원들을 돕습니까?
   A : 지휘자는 연주자들을 이끌고, 제때 연주할 수 있도록 도와줍니다.

Step 4   교과서 받아쓰기   p. 85

An Orchestra

The members of all the families of instruments – percussion, string, wind, and brass – come together in an orchestra. It takes many musicians playing many instruments to make up an orchestra.

An orchestra has a conductor. The conductor does not play an instrument. The conductor is a man or woman who stands in front of the orchestra and helps the musicians stay together and play when they are supposed to. The conductor is like the coach of a team: he or she makes sure that all the members of the orchestra play their best and do their job at the right time.

To show respect, people sometimes address the conductor as "maestro," which means "master."

✳ 지문 해석

관현악단

관현악단에는 모든 악기군 – 타악기, 현악기, 목관악기, 금관악기 – 이 함께 모여 있습니다. 관현악단을 구성하기 위해서는 많은 악기를 연주하는 연주자들이 많이 필요합니다.

관현악단에는 지휘자가 있습니다. 지휘자는 악기를 연주하지 않죠. 지휘자는 관현악단 앞에 서서 연주자들을 이끌고, 연주해야 할 때에 연주할 수 있도록 도와주는 남자 또는 여자입니다. 지휘자는 한 팀의 감독과도 같습니다: 지휘자는 관현악단의 모든 단원들이 반드시 최고의 기량을 발휘하고, 제때 연주할 수 있도록 합니다.

존경을 표하는 의미에서, 때때로 사람들은 지휘자를 '마에스트로' 라고 부르는데, 이 말은 '거장' 이라는 뜻입니다.

Unit **14**

Great Composers and a Symphony

Step 1 | 단어 받아쓰기   p. 88

❶ piece   작품, 조각
❷ composer   작곡가
❸ symphony   교향곡
❹ classical   고전적인, 고전의
❺ way   방식
❻ special   특별한
❼ movement   악장, 움직임
❽ divide   나누다
❾ known   알려진
❿ quite   꽤

Step 2 | 문장 받아쓰기   p. 89

1단계 느린 속도로 듣고 받아쓰기

❶ It is a piece of music written for an orchestra to play.
❷ A symphony is a very special kind of classical music.
❸ Joseph Haydn is known as the "Father of the Symphony."
❹ The beginning of Beethoven's *Fifth Symphony* is one of the most famous movements in all of classical music.

2단계 정상 속도로 듣고 받아쓰기

❶ Joseph Haydn is known as the "Father of the Symphony."
❷ A symphony is a very special kind of classical music.
❸ The beginning of Beethoven's *Fifth Symphony* is one of the most famous movements in all of classical music.
❹ It is a piece of music written for an orchestra to play.

Step 3 | 대화문 받아쓰기   p. 90

❶ Q : Does it take long to listen to an entire symphony?
    A : Yes, a symphony is quite a long piece of music.
❷ Q : What is music by Mozart, Bach, and Beethoven called?
    A : Their music is called classical music.
❸ Q : How famous is the beginning of Beethoven's *Fifth Symphony*?
    A : It is one of the most famous movements in all of classical music.
❹ Q : How many symphonies did Mozart write?
    A : He wrote forty-one symphonies.

＊ 대화문 받아쓰기 해석

❶ Q : 교향곡 전곡을 듣는 데 긴 시간이 필요한가요?
    A : 네, 교향곡은 꽤 긴 음악 작품입니다.
❷ Q : 모차르트, 바흐, 베토벤의 음악을 무엇이라고 하나요?
    A : 그들의 음악을 고전음악이라고 합니다.
❸ Q : 베토벤의 〈5번 교향곡〉 도입부는 얼마나 유명한가요?
    A : 그것은 모든 고전음악 중에서 가장 유명한 악장 중의 하나입니다.
❹ Q : 모차르트는 얼마나 많은 교향곡을 썼나요?
    A : 그는 41개의 교향곡을 썼습니다.

Step 4 | 교과서 받아쓰기   p. 91

Great Composers and a Symphony

Music by composers such as Mozart, Bach,

Beethoven, and Tchaikovsky is called classical music.

A symphony is a very special kind of classical music. It is a piece of music written for an orchestra to play. It may be quite a long piece—sometimes half an hour or more. It is divided into parts—usually 3 or 4 parts of them. They are called movements. There are lots of different ways of writing a symphony.

Mozart wrote forty-one symphonies. Beethoven wrote nine great symphonies. The beginning of Beethoven's *Fifth Symphony* is one of the most famous movements in all of classical music. Joseph Haydn is known as the "Father of the Symphony."

* 지문 해석

위대한 작곡가와 교향곡

모차르트, 바흐, 베토벤, 그리고 차이코프스키와 같은 작곡가들의 음악을 고전음악이라고 합니다.

교향곡은 매우 특별한 유형의 고전음악입니다. 교향곡은 관현악단이 연주할 수 있도록 쓴 음악 작품입니다. 교향곡은 꽤 길 수도 있는데, 때때로 30분이나 그 이상이 되기도 합니다. 교향곡은 몇 부분으로 나누어지는데, 대개 3개 또는 4개 부분으로 나뉩니다. 그것을 악장이라고 합니다.

교향곡을 작곡하는 방식은 다양합니다. 모차르트는 41개의 교향곡을 썼습니다. 베토벤은 9개의 위대한 교향곡을 썼죠. 베토벤의 〈5번 교향곡〉 도입부는 모든 고전음악 중에서 가장 유명한 악장 중의 하나입니다. 요제프 하이든은 '교향곡의 아버지'로 알려져 있습니다.

Unit 15

Opera

Step 1   단어 받아쓰기   p. 94

❶ play   연극

❷ composer   작곡가
❸ language   언어
❹ opera   오페라
❺ stage   무대
❻ instead   대신에
❼ costume   의상, 복장
❽ actor   배우
❾ line   대사
❿ perform   공연하다

Step 2   문장 받아쓰기   p. 95

1단계 느린 속도로 듣고 받아쓰기

❶ Many operas were written by composers who lived in European countries, such as Italy, Germany, and France.

❷ In an opera, the actors sing and act out the story on the stage, too, but they do not speak their lines.

❸ An opera is like a play in which everything is sung instead of spoken.

❹ While they sing, an orchestra plays music for them to sing along with.

2단계 정상 속도로 듣고 받아쓰기

❶ An opera is like a play in which everything is sung instead of spoken.

❷ In an opera, the actors sing and act out the story on the stage, too, but they do not speak their lines.

❸ While they sing, an orchestra plays music for them to sing along with.

❹ Many operas were written by composers who lived in European countries, such as Italy, Germany, and France.

Step 3   대화문 받아쓰기   p. 96

❶ Q : In an opera, who plays music while the actors sing?

A : An orchestra plays music.

❷ Q : In an opera, is everything sung?

A : Yes, everything is sung instead of spoken.

❸ Q : Why do many people love operas even though they do not understand them?

A : Because the singing and music are so beautiful.

❹ Q : Where were many opera composers from?

A : They were from European countries.

＊대화문 받아쓰기 해석

❶ Q : 오페라에서는 배우들이 노래하는 동안에 누가 음악을 연주하나요?

A : 관현악단이 음악을 연주합니다.

❷ Q : 오페라에서는 모든 것을 노래로 하나요?

A : 네, 모든 것을 말 대신에 노래로 합니다.

❸ Q : 왜 많은 사람들이 오페라를 잘 이해하지 못하면서도 오페라를 사랑하나요?

A : 노래와 음악이 매우 아름답기 때문입니다.

❹ Q : 많은 오페라 작곡가들은 어디 출신이었나요?

A : 그들은 유럽 국가 출신이었습니다.

Step 4 　교과서 받아쓰기　　　p. 97

Opera

An opera is like a play in which everything is sung instead of spoken. In a play, people put on costumes and then go onstage to act out a story.

In an opera, the actors sing and act out the story on the stage, too, but they do not speak their lines. And while they sing, an orchestra plays music for them to sing along with. Operas are usually performed in opera houses.

Many operas were written by composers who lived in European countries, such as Italy, Germany, and France. That is why many operas are sung in other languages than English. But because the singing and music are so beautiful, many people love to listen to operas even if they do not understand all the words.

＊지문 해석

오페라

오페라는 모든 것을 말 대신에 노래로 하는 연극과도 같습니다. 연극에서 사람들은 의상을 입고 무대로 나가 줄거리를 연기합니

다.

마찬가지로, 오페라에서도 배우들이 무대에서 노래를 부르고 줄거리를 연기하지만, 그들은 대사를 말하지 않죠. 그리고 그들이 노래하는 동안에, 관현악단은 배우들이 음악에 맞춰 노래할 수 있도록 음악을 연주합니다. 오페라는 보통 오페라 하우스에서 공연합니다.

많은 오페라가 이탈리아와 독일, 그리고 프랑스와 같은 유럽 국가에 살았던 작곡가들에 의해 쓰여졌습니다. 이것이 바로, 오페라가 영어가 아닌 다른 언어로 불리는 이유입니다. 하지만 노래와 음악이 매우 아름답기 때문에, 모든 말을 다 알아듣지는 못할지언정 많은 사람들이 오페라 듣는 것을 사랑합니다.

Unit 16

Ballet

Step 1 　단어 받아쓰기　　　p. 100

❶ ballet 　　　　발레
❷ spin 　　　　돌다, 회전하다
❸ tip 　　　　끝
❹ leap 　　　　높이뛰기, 도약
❺ training 　　　　훈련
❻ balance 　　　　균형을 유지하다
❼ control 　　　　통제하다, 조절하다
❽ practice 　　　　연습하다
❾ beauty 　　　　아름다움, 미인
❿ air 　　　　공중, 허공

Step 2 　문장 받아쓰기　　　p. 101

1단계 　느린 속도로 듣고 받아쓰기

❶ Ballet can tell a story.

❷ Sometimes they make high leaps into the air.

❸ Ballet dancers have to practice for years to learn all they need to know.

❹ Instead, in many ballets, the dancers tell a story through the way they move.

18

❶ Ballet can tell a story.

❷ Instead, in many ballets, the dancers tell a story through the way they move.

❸ Ballet dancers have to practice for years to learn all they need to know.

❹ Sometimes they make high leaps into the air.

Step 3 대화문 받아쓰기 — p. 102

❶ Q : How do ballet dancers tell a story?
  A : They tell a story through the way they move.

❷ Q : Is ballet a type of dance or music?
  A : It is a type of dance.

❸ Q : Why do ballet dancers have to work at controlling their bodies?
  A : Because sometimes they spin around and around.

❹ Q : Why do ballet dancers have to work at balancing themselves?
  A : Because sometimes they dance only on the tips of their toes.

＊ 대화문 받아쓰기 해석

❶ Q : 발레 무용수들은 어떻게 이야기를 전달할 수 있나요?
  A : 그들은 움직임을 통해 이야기를 전달합니다.

❷ Q : 발레는 춤이나 음악의 한 종류입니까?
  A : 그것은 춤의 한 종류입니다.

❸ Q : 왜 발레 무용수들은 몸을 조절하는 연습을 해야 하나요?
  A : 그들은 때때로 몸을 계속 회전해야 하기 때문입니다.

❹ Q : 왜 발레 무용수들은 균형을 유지하는 연습을 해야 하나요?
  A : 때로 그들은 발끝으로만 춤을 추어야 하기 때문입니다.

Step 4 교과서 받아쓰기 — p. 103

Ballet

Ballet is a type of dance. It is only done by dancers who have had special training.

Ballet can tell a story. In a ballet, there is music, often played by an orchestra, but no one sings or talks. Instead, in many ballets, the dancers tell a story through the way they move. Some ballets tell stories you may know, like the story of *Sleeping Beauty*.

Ballet dancers have to practice for years to learn all they need to know. They have to work very hard and have very strong legs. They have to work at balancing themselves and controlling their bodies. Sometimes they dance only on the tips of their toes. Sometimes they spin around and around. Sometimes they make high leaps into the air.

＊ 지문 해석

발레

발레는 춤의 한 종류입니다. 발레는 특별한 훈련을 받은 무용수들만이 춥니다.

발레는 이야기를 전달할 수 있습니다. 발레에는 음악이 있는데, 대개는 관현악단이 연주하지만, 아무도 노래하거나 말하지 않습니다. 대신에, 많은 발레에서 무용수들은 움직임을 통해 이야기를 전달합니다. 어떤 발레는 〈잠자는 숲 속의 공주〉처럼 사람들이 알 만한 이야기를 들려주기도 합니다.

발레 무용수들은 알아야 하는 모든 것을 배우기 위해 수 년 동안 연습해야 합니다. 그들은 열심히 연습해야만 하고 매우 튼튼한 다리를 가져야 합니다. 균형을 유지하고 몸을 조절하는 연습을 해야 하는 것이죠. 때로 그들은 발끝으로만 춤을 추기도 합니다. 어떨 때는 몸을 계속 회전하기도 하죠. 때때로 그들은 공중으로 높이 뛰어오르기도 합니다.

Unit 17

Shapes

Step 1 단어 받아쓰기 — p. 106

❶ square   정사각형
❷ oval   타원형
❸ triangle   삼각형, 세모
❹ point   꼭짓점

⑤ rest   정지해 있다, 쉬다
⑥ shape   모양, 형태
⑦ rectangle   직사각형
⑧ join   연결하다
⑨ circle   원, 동그라미
⑩ diamond   마름모, 다이아몬드

Step 2   문장 받아쓰기   p. 107

1단계 느린 속도로 듣고 받아쓰기

❶ Circles roll and make you think of wheels, marbles, and balls.
❷ Triangles have points, and the points can make you think of something moving in a certain direction, like a rocket rising into the sky.
❸ Squares and rectangles seem to rest in one place and make you think of big rectangular objects, like refrigerators.
❹ When lines join together, they make shapes.

2단계 정상 속도로 듣고 받아쓰기

❶ When lines join together, they make shapes.
❷ Circles roll and make you think of wheels, marbles, and balls.
❸ Squares and rectangles seem to rest in one place and make you think of big rectangular objects, like refrigerators.
❹ Triangles have points, and the points can make you think of something moving in a certain direction, like a rocket rising into the sky.

Step 3   대화문 받아쓰기   p. 108

❶ Q : What can make you think of refrigerators?
   A : Squares and rectangles.
❷ Q : What can make you think of wheels, marbles, and balls?
   A : A circle.
❸ Q : What can different shapes make you feel and think?
   A : They can make us feel and think different things.

❹ Q : What do shapes come from?
   A : They come from lines.

✳ 대화문 받아쓰기 해석

❶ Q : 무엇이 여러분으로 하여금 냉장고를 떠올릴 수 있도록 합니까?
   A : 정사각형과 직사각형입니다.
❷ Q : 무엇이 여러분으로 하여금 바퀴와 구슬, 공을 생각날 수 있도록 합니까?
   A : 원입니다.
❸ Q : 서로 다른 도형은 여러분으로 하여금 무엇을 느끼고 생각하게 합니까?
   A : 그것들은 우리에게 서로 다른 느낌과 생각을 줄 수 있습니다.
❹ Q : 도형은 무엇으로부터 만들어지나요?
   A : 도형은 선으로부터 만들어집니다.

Step 4   교과서 받아쓰기   p. 109

Shapes

When lines join together, they make shapes. Here are three shapes: a circle, a square, and a triangle. Here are three other shapes: a rectangle, an oval, and a diamond.
Different shapes can sometimes make you feel and think different things. Look again at the circle and the square. Which one makes you think of something moving? Circles roll and can make you think of wheels, marbles, and balls. Squares and rectangles seem to rest in one place and can make you think of big rectangular objects, like refrigerators. Triangles have points, and the points can make you think of something moving in a certain direction, like a rocket rising into the sky.

✳ 지문 해석

여러 가지 도형

몇 개의 선이 만나면, 도형을 만듭니다. 여기 세 가지의 도형이 있습니다: 원, 정사각형, 삼각형. 다음은 또 다른 세 가지 도형입니다: 직사각형, 타원, 마름모.
서로 다른 도형은 여러분에게 서로 다른 느낌과 생각을 줄 수 있습니다. 원과 정사각형을 다시 한 번 보세요. 여러분으로 하여금 움직이는 어떤 것을 떠올리게 하는 도형은 어떤 것인가요? 원은 굴러가기 때문에 바퀴와 구슬, 공을 생각나게 할 수 있습니다. 정사각형과 직사각형은 한 곳에 정지해 있는 것처럼 보이기 때문에, 여러분이 냉장고와 같은 큰 직사각형을 떠올리도록 합니다. 삼각형은 꼭짓점이 있어서, 그 꼭짓점은 여러분으로 하여금 하늘로 날아오르는 로켓처럼 특정한 방향으로 움직이는 것을 떠올리게 할 수 있습니다.

Unit 18

Portraits

Step 1 단어 받아쓰기
p. 112

❶ shelf	선반
❷ face	얼굴
❸ portrait	초상화
❹ artist	예술가, 화가
❺ Italian	이탈리아의; 이탈리아인
❻ paint	(색을 칠해) 그리다
❼ draw	(선으로) 그리다
❽ picture	사진, 그림
❾ fascinate	마음을 빼앗다, 매료시키다
❿ expression	표현, 표정

Step 2 문장 받아쓰기
p. 113

1단계 느린 속도로 듣고 받아쓰기

❶ Portraits can tell a lot about a person and the time in which he or she lived.

❷ A portrait is what we call a picture of a person.

❸ Perhaps the most famous portrait in the world is *The Mona Lisa*.

❹ Portraits can be taken with cameras, or they can be drawn or painted.

2단계 정상 속도로 듣고 받아쓰기

❶ Portraits can be taken with cameras, or they can be drawn or painted.

❷ Portraits can tell a lot about a person and the time in which he or she lived.

❸ A portrait is what we call a picture of a person.

❹ Perhaps the most famous portrait in the world is *The Mona Lisa*.

Step 3 대화문 받아쓰기
p. 114

❶ Q : Who painted *The Mona Lisa*?

   A : The Italian artist Leonardo da Vinci painted *The Mona Lisa*.

❷ Q : What has fascinated people about *The Mona Lisa* for a long time?

   A : The expression on *The Mona Lisa*'s face.

❸ Q : What do you call a picture of you on the wall?

   A : We call it a portrait.

❹ Q : Can portraits be drawn?

   A : Yes, and they also can be painted or taken with cameras.

* 대화문 받아쓰기 해석

❶ Q : 누가 〈모나리자〉를 그렸나요?

   A : 이탈리아의 화가 레오나르도 다 빈치가 〈모나리자〉를 그렸습니다.

❷ Q : 수백 년 동안 사람들은 〈모나리자〉의 무엇에 매료됐나요?

   A : 〈모나리자〉의 얼굴에 드러난 표정입니다.

❸ Q : 여러분은 벽에 걸린 당신의 사진을 무엇이라고 하나요?

   A : 우리는 그것을 초상화라고 합니다.

❹ Q : 초상화는 선으로 그릴 수 있나요?

   A : 네, 그것들은 또한 색을 칠해 그리거나 사진으로 찍을 수도 있습니다.

Step 4 교과서 받아쓰기
p. 115

Portraits

Have you had your picture taken at school? Or is there a picture of you on a wall or shelf at home? That's your portrait. That's what we call a picture of a person. Portraits can be taken with cameras, or

they can be drawn or painted.
Perhaps the most famous portrait in the world is
The Mona Lisa. It was painted by the Italian artist
Leonardo da Vinci about five hundred years ago.
Look at the expression on *The Mona Lisa*'s
face. For hundreds of years, people have been
fascinated by her expression. What do you think
she might be thinking? Portraits can tell a lot about
a person and the time in which he or she lived.

＊지문 해석

초상화

학교에서 당신의 사진을 찍은 적이 있나요? 아니면, 집의 벽이나
선반에 당신의 사진이 걸려 있나요? 그것이 바로 당신의 초상화입
니다. 초상화는 한 인물의 사진[그림]을 일컫는 것입니다. 초상화
는 사진으로 찍거나 그림으로 그릴 수도 있습니다.
세상에서 가장 유명한 초상화는 아마도 〈모나리자〉일 것입니다.
모나리자는 오백 년 전에 이탈리아의 화가 레오나르도 다 빈치가
그렸습니다.
모나리자 얼굴에 드러난 표정을 보세요. 수백 년 동안 사람들은
〈모나리자〉의 표정에 매료되어 왔습니다. 모나리자가 무엇을 생
각하는 것 같나요? 초상화는 한 사람과 그가 살았던 시대에 대해
많은 것을 말해 줄 수 있습니다.

Unit 19

Self-Portraits

Step.1   단어 받아쓰기   p. 118

❶ painter   화가
❷ Dutch   네덜란드의; 네덜란드인
❸ feeling   느낌
❹ self-portrait   자화상
❺ worried   근심스러운
❻ photograph   사진
❼ show   나타내다
❽ idea   아이디어, 발상

❾ triple   3배의, 셋으로 된
❿ calm   차분한

Step 2   문장 받아쓰기   p. 119

1단계 느린 속도로 듣고 받아쓰기

❶ The Dutch painter Vincent van Gogh painted 37
self-portraits.
❷ You get a very different feeling from a self-
portrait painted by American artist Norman
Rockwell.
❸ A self-portrait does not have to look like a
photograph.
❹ Sometimes an artist paints a portrait of himself.

2단계 정상 속도로 듣고 받아쓰기

❶ Sometimes an artist paints a portrait of himself.
❷ A self-portrait does not have to look like a
photograph.
❸ The Dutch painter Vincent van Gogh painted 37
self-portraits.
❹ You get a very different feeling from a self-
portrait painted by American artist Norman
Rockwell.

Step 3   대화문 받아쓰기   p. 120

❶ Q : Does each portrait of a person say
       something different?
   A : Yes, it says something different about the
       way he feels about himself.
❷ Q : Should I paint myself the same way as
       photographs?
   A : No. You can paint yourself in different ways.
❸ Q : In *Triple Self-Portrait*, how many self-
       portraits did Norman Rockwell paint?
   A : Three self-portraits.
❹ Q : Did van Gogh paint himself often?
   A : Yes, he painted 37 self-portraits.

＊대화문 받아쓰기 해석

❶ Q : 사람의 각각의 초상화는 다른 것을 말해주나요?

22

A : 네, 그것은 자신을 어떻게 다르게 느끼는지를 말해줍니다.
❷ Q : 저는 저 자신을 사진처럼 보이도록 그려야 하나요?
A : 아니요. 당신은 매우 다양한 방식으로 자신을 그릴 수 있습니다.
❸ Q : 〈3개의 자화상〉에서 노만 록웰은 얼마나 많은 자화상을 그렸나요?
A : 세 개입니다.
❹ Q : 반 고흐는 종종 자신을 그렸나요?
A : 네, 그는 37점의 자화상을 그렸습니다.

Step 4 교과서 받아쓰기 p. 121

Self-Portraits

Sometimes an artist paints a portrait of himself. This is called a self-portrait. A self-portrait does not have to look like a photograph. You can paint yourself in many different ways, and each way will say something different about the way you feel about yourself.

The Dutch painter Vincent van Gogh painted 37 self-portraits. This one, called *Self-Portrait*, shows him when he was thirty-six years old. How does van Gogh look to you? Does he seem calm or worried?

You get a very different feeling from a self-portrait painted by American artist Norman Rockwell. In this painting, called *Triple Self-Portrait*, Rockwell has fun with the idea of painting a picture of himself. How many times does Rockwell show himself here?

＊ 지문 해석

자화상

때때로 화가는 자신의 초상화를 그리기도 합니다. 이것은 '자화상'이라고 부릅니다. 자화상은 반드시 사진처럼 보일 필요는 없습니다. 당신은 매우 다양한 방식으로 스스로를 그릴 수 있고, 각각의 방식은 당신이 스스로를 어떻게 느끼는지를 말해 줄 것입니다. 네덜란드 화가 빈센트 반 고흐는 37점의 자화상을 그렸습니다. 〈자화상〉이라고 불리는 이 작품은 36세 때의 화가 자신을 보여주고 있습니다. 당신에게는 고흐가 어때 보이나요? 차분해 보이나요? 아니면 걱정스러워 보이나요?

미국의 화가 노만 록웰이 그린 자화상을 보면, 매우 다른 느낌을

받게 됩니다. 〈3개의 자화상〉이라고 불리는 이 그림에서, 록웰은 재미있는 아이디어로 자신을 그렸습니다. 이 자화상에서 록웰은 자신을 몇 번이나 나타내고 있나요?

Unit 20

Still Lifes

Step 1 단어 받아쓰기 p. 124

❶ popular   인기 있는
❷ raise   올리다, 인상하다
❸ texture   질감, 결
❹ still life   정물, 정물화
❺ arrange   배치하다, 정렬하다
❻ include   포함하다
❼ china   도자기
❽ furniture   가구
❾ fine art   예술
❿ object   물체, 물건

Step 2 문장 받아쓰기 p. 125

1단계 느린 속도로 듣고 받아쓰기

❶ People are not included in a still life.
❷ It is called a still life because the objects in the painting do not move.
❸ Once the artist knows what to paint, he or she has to decide how to arrange the objects.
❹ To paint a still life, an artist first has to decide what objects to paint.

2단계 정상 속도로 듣고 받아쓰기

❶ To paint a still life, an artist first has to decide what objects to paint.
❷ Once the artist knows what to paint, he or she has to decide how to arrange the objects.

23

❸ People are not included in a still life.
❹ It is called a still life because the objects in the painting do not move.

Step 3   대화문 받아쓰기   p. 126

❶ Q: Where does the term still life come from?
   A: It comes from the fact that the objects in the painting do not move.
❷ Q: Since when has still-life painting been popular?
   A: It has been popular since the 17th century.
❸ Q: Who raised still-life painting to a fine art?
   A: Dutch painters.
❹ Q: How many people can we see in a still life?
   A: People are not included in a still life.

＊ 대화문 받아쓰기 해석
❶ Q: 정물화라는 용어는 어디에서 왔나요?
   A: 그것은 그림 속의 물체가 움직이지 않는다는 사실에서 왔습니다.
❷ Q: 정물화는 언제부터 인기를 얻었나요?
   A: 그것은 17세기 이래로 인기를 얻었습니다.
❸ Q: 누가 정물화를 예술로 끌어올렸나요?
   A: 네덜란드 화가들입니다.
❹ Q: 우리는 정물화에서 얼마나 많은 사람을 볼 수 있나요?
   A: 사람은 정물화에 포함되지 않습니다.

Step 4   교과서 받아쓰기   p. 127

Still Lifes

There is a kind of painting called a still life. It is called a still life because the objects in the painting do not move. People are not included in a still life. Still-life painting has been popular since the 17th century, when Dutch painters raised it to a fine art. To paint a still life, an artist first has to decide what objects to paint. Still lifes often include flowers, fruit, books, china, silverware, furniture, or other small objects. Once the artist knows what to paint, he or she has to decide how to arrange the objects. What shapes and colors will go next to

one another? Where will the light fall? Will the still life include objects with several different textures?

＊ 지문 해석

정물화
'정물화'라고 불리는 그림의 일종이 있습니다. 그림 속의 물체가 움직이지 않기 때문에 정물화라고 불립니다. 사람은 정물화의 대상에 포함되지 않습니다.
정물화는 17세기 이래로 인기를 얻고 있는데, 네덜란드의 화가들이 정물화를 예술로 끌어올렸습니다.
정물화를 그리기 위해서 화가는 먼저 어떤 물체를 그릴 것인지 결정해야 합니다. 정물화에는 꽃과 과일, 책, 도자기, 은식기, 가구 또는 다른 작은 물체들이 자주 포함됩니다. 일단 화가가 무엇을 그릴지 안다면, 그는 물체를 어떻게 배치할 것인지 결정해야 합니다. 이 물체 옆에는 어떤 모양과 색깔을 둘까? 빛은 어디에 떨어지게 할까? 다양한 질감을 가진 물체를 정물화에 포함시킬까?

리스닝 with DICTATION

Level 3

미국교과서 지문 듣기로 귀가 열리면 영어에 대한 자신감 상승

1 과학, 사회, 음악, 미술의 미국 초등학교 교과서 지문을 듣고, 받아쓰면 듣기 실력 향상은 물론 다양한 교과 지식을 얻을 수 있습니다.

2 단어와 문장을 들으면서 단어 받아쓰기 → 문장 받아쓰기 → 대화문 받아쓰기 → 교과서 받아쓰기의 단계를 따라 학습하다 보면 교과서의 단어와 문장을 자연스럽게 외우게 됩니다.

3 학습자가 스스로 듣고, 따라 말하고, 받아쓰며 정답을 확인하는 과정을 통해서 듣기 실력은 물론 말하기, 쓰기, 읽기의 통합적 영어 실력을 키울 수 있습니다.

★ 미국교과서 리스닝 with DICTATION 시리즈 ★

단계	수록 과목	지문 당 단어	권장 학년
Level 1	과학, 사회, 음악, 미술	60 단어	초등 4학년
Level 2	과학, 사회, 음악, 미술	60~100 단어	초등 5학년
Level 3	**과학, 사회, 음악, 미술**	**100~120 단어**	**초등 6학년**

부가자료 다운로드 서비스

www.gilbutschool.co.kr

• MP3 파일
• Word List & Test (영한 / 한영)
• Key Sentence Writing & Translation